ELECTRIC FRANCHISES IN NEW YORK CITY

BY

LEONORA ARENT, M. A.

Professor of Economics in Saint Mary-of-the-Woods College

SUBMITTED IN PARTIAL FULFILMENT OF THE REQUIREMENTS
FOR THE DEGREE OF DOCTOR OF PHILOSOPHY
IN THE
FACULTY OF POLITICAL SCIENCE
COLUMBIA UNIVERSITY

NEW YORK
1919

To

MY MOTHER AND FATHER

PREFACE

To ascertain the status of the franchises held by the electric-lighting companies of New York City is the purpose of this study. In 1910 Mr. Milo R. Maltbie, then a member of the Public Service Commission for the First District, submitted to the Commission a report on the franchises of electrical corporations in Greater New York, analyzing the franchises granted by the different political subdivisions now consolidated in Greater New York, and setting forth the existing rights and obligations of the electric light companies. Since then litigation has been in progress regarding the validity of important franchises, and changes in intercorporate relations have been effected by a recent merger. This study devotes attention as well to the subjects of franchise by acquiescence and of the duration of grants in which no time limit is expressed.

Records in the Bureau of Real Estate of Corporations and Special Franchises in the Department of Taxes and Assessments of New York City and reports of the electric-lighting companies to the Public Service Commission have been consulted for data concerning the special franchise valuations discussed in the opening chapter. Mr. M. S. Howard, an accountant of the Public Service Commission, has rendered assistance in interpreting the reports of the companies. Helpful suggestions have been received from the Bureau of Special Franchises of the State Tax Department. In particular, the writer acknowledges indebtedness to Professor E. R. A. Seligman for the help received from his lectures on taxation.

Access to the Public Service Commission's files in its Franchise Bureau and Filing Department has facilitated the compiling of material. For the many courtesies extended by Mr. L. G. Benedict, of Counsel for the Consolidated Gas Company of New York, Mr. W. J. Meyers, Secretary of the United Electric Light and Power Company, and Mr. Vincent Victory, Assistant Corporation Counsel for the City of New York, the writer expresses appreciation. The writer is under heaviest obligations to Professor Howard Lee McBain, whose valuable time has been given with the utmost generosity in guidance and constructive criticism throughout the preparation of this study.

ERRATA.

P. 46, line 17, for "than" read "then".
P. 108, line 6, for "four" read "three".

CONTENTS

PAGE

CHAPTER I

Electric Lighting Companies of New York City

CHAPTER II

Franchises Claimed by Operating Companies

CHAPTER III

Doubtful and Invalid Franchises

CHAPTER IV

The General Manufacturing Corporations Act

CHAPTER V

The Problems of Acquiescence and Perpetuity

CHAPTER I

Electric-Lighting Companies of New York City

With the national government's assumption of control of many industries after the entrance of this country into the war, public attention was directed toward the possibility or probability of permanent government ownership upon the return to peace conditions. Consideration of the relative merits of public and private ownership became charged with local interest for the citizens of New York City when the demand for municipal ownership of public utilities was made a plank in the platform of the Democratic party both in the mayoralty campaign of 1917 and in the 1918 campaign which resulted in the election of Alfred E. Smith as Democratic governor. " Home rule for municipalities, including full right to own and operate their public utilities " was the Democratic slogan.[1] Accordingly, in his inaugural speech of January 1, 1919, Governor Smith presented the views of his party in the following words: [2]

Recent years have been marked by a great opening of the popular mind to the true scope of enlightened municipal administration. There is everywhere a recognition that it is only through the application of progressive conceptions of public duty that life can be made tolerable in our teeming cities, with their unprecedented growth in population, and the consequent living conditions. From every city in the state, represented by

[1] *Democratic state platform,* adopted at Saratoga Springs, July 23, 1918.

[2] *The New York Times*, January 2, 1919, p. 4.

their chief executives in conference, there comes the demand that the State confer upon the cities the power to acquire, own, operate, and control their public utilities. The supply of transportation, light, heat and power, is of the utmost importance to each local community. The services rendered have become a necessity to the life, health, comfort, convenience, and industry of the cities. These great services are monopolies, and whatever is of necessity a monopoly should be a public monopoly, especially where it offers a service of universal use. I therefore recommend that legislation be passed granting our cities the power to acquire, own, operate, and control their public utilities.

Decidedly adverse comment on the remarks of the governor was immediately expressed by an independent Democratic paper of New York City: [1]

Since Governor Smith has to deal with a Republican legislature, a sort of unreality makes itself felt in his first message . . . But how painful to find him talking about "the true scope of enlightened municipal administration," and approving the effort of the singularly bedarkened municipal administration of this city to set up municipal ownership and operation. This scheme, financially impossible, the governor recommends to the legislature, well knowing that it is the last thing the legislature will do.

This study makes no pretentious claim to set forth a general statement regarding the defects or merits of municipal ownership of public utilities with reference to all our cities or one. Apart from such theoretical arguments as the right of a city to control its own streets in the interest of its own citizens rather than to submit to the occupancy of its highways as a property right held by a private monopoly for private gain, it would be a barren task to attempt to arrive

[1] *The New York Times*, January 2, 1919, p. 8.

at worth-while conclusions concerning the relative merits of private and public ownership of public utilities as a whole. It would be almost as fruitless to attempt to generalize on the subject as applicable to a single utility in all cities. Even when consideration is limited to but one class of public utilities and one city, judgment should be reached only after careful investigation of facts. Conclusions drawn from examples of municipal ownership on both sides of the Atlantic are used both in support and attack of the policy. Enthusiasts for municipal ownership of public utilities find excuses for every apparent failure of its application, and paint in glowing colors instances of its success which they allege show increased efficiency of service, improved conditions of the utility employees, and separation of the utilities from politics. Opponents array facts to justify conclusions inimical to the cause of municipal ownership. A middle ground is indeed held by some who hope for eventual municipal ownership of public utilities, but who appreciate the significance of differences among places as to social, economic and political conditions, and who hesitate, therefore, to concede that because municipal ownership succeeds in one section, it must in another. Each city must be studied by itself, in the light of its own particular problems. Whether or not the city of New York would promote the interests of its inhabitants by municipal ownership of electric-lighting utilities, is a question apart. In view, however, of the increased agitation for municipal ownership,[1] the

[1] Legislative Index Publishing Company, *Record of all Bills Introduced in the Senate and Assembly during the 142d Annual Session of the Legislature of the State of New York, Beginning January 1, 1919.* Between January 1, 1919 and March 6, 1919, five bills providing for municipal ownership of public utilities were introduced in the Senate, printed Senate numbers, 65, 179, 301, 805, 806, respectively; and five were introduced in the Assembly, printed Assembly numbers, 180, 415, 434, 1103, 1229, respectively.

primary purpose of this study is to ascertain the present status of the franchise rights of the electric-lighting companies in the city of New York.

Before going into the fuller discussion of the franchises held or claimed by the electric-lighting companies of the city of New York, it seems desirable to consider the meaning of the term *franchise*. A franchise has been comprehensively defined as a right conferred by government of conducting an occupation either in a particular way or accompanied with particular privileges.[1] It is correct to speak of the state as the primary franchise-granting authority. In the case of the electric-lighting companies of the city of New York, the original grantees of the municipal franchises now held by the operating companies received from the state the corporate or general franchise which conferred the right to be or to become and the right to do; and they obtained from the political subdivision in question the right to occupy the streets in the pursuit of their business. The last-named, intangible right is designated a municipal franchise. In the analysis of the franchises of the electric-lighting companies of the city of New York, attention will be constantly directed to the fact that the original grantee obtained rights to occupy the streets of a given territory from boards of aldermen, common councils, highway commissioners, boards of parks, town boards, or boards of supervisors. Clearly, the state has supreme authority over the use of the streets and public highways. Except as otherwise provided in the state constitution, this power is vested in the legislature, and the legislature, in turn, through statutory enactment or charter provisions, or both, delegates to the local authorities of the political subdivision the power to grant the municipal franchise.

In the case of the street railroads in the city of New York

[1] Seligman, *Essays on Taxation*, p. 221.

there has been, since 1875, a somewhat distinctive factor. Section 18 of the third article of the constitution of the state provides in part as follows:

No law shall authorize the construction or operation of a street railroad except upon the condition that the consent . . . also of the local authorities having control of that portion of a street or highway upon which it is proposed to construct or operate such railroad be first obtained.

Discussing the significance of this provision, a former attorney for the public service commission for the first district says in part: [1]

The Constitution clothes the City with an independent legislative power and discretion, a delegation *pro tanto* of the State's sovereign powers. This is very different from saying that the *legislature's* powers have been delegated to the city, as is the case where the delegation is by legislative act rather than constitutional grant. The City is by the Constitution made "an independent contractor" with respect to a street railroad corporation's invasion of public streets, and not merely "an agent of the legislature," as it is probably to be deemed to be when acting under a statutory provision for municipal consent.

Interpreted in the light of both the general character of the corporate franchise and the delegation of power by the state, the seemingly uncertain expressions frequently used in designating a municipal franchise gather more clarity of meaning. To use the term *secondary franchise* is but to stress the primary franchise-granting authority of the state. The term *particular franchise* merely emphasizes the general character of the authorization conferred by the corporate or general franchise. Needless confusion, however,

[1] Ransom, Copy of brief filed in the court of appeals in the case of Quinby *v.* Public Service Commission, Second District, p. 79.

results from attempting to attach peculiar significance to the word *consent*, as though that word literally made the city's contract with the company something inferior to a real municipal franchise. To ignore or minimize the authority of the city to give or withhold its consent to the occupancy of its streets, and to emphasize only the state's or the legislature's indisputably important share in the process of franchise-granting is without justification. Sometimes the effect of the city's consent is explained by saying that the local authority is vested with the power to give the consent requisite to confer a franchise upon the corporation concerned. Others phrase their interpretation of the city's consent by maintaining that the consent, when given, becomes a franchise granted to the corporation. It would seem that the essential idea underlying the use of such expressions is to draw a distinction between the right to occupy certain streets or certain areas as made possible by the city's consent, and the right to become or do, as conferred by the corporate and general franchise. It is perfectly evident that the right to become or do is worthless without the right to occupy the streets.

There are five boroughs in the city of New York: Manhattan, The Bronx, Queens, Brooklyn, and Richmond. The area of the city is 314.75 square miles; the estimated population in 1918 was 5,872,143.[1] Three companies furnish electric lighting in the borough of Manhattan,[2] namely, the

[1] *Report of Taxes and Assessments of the City of New York*, 1918, p. 16.

[2] A fourth company, the Riverside Light and Power Company, supplies electricity in the section bounded by 130th street, 132d street, Twelfth avenue, and the tracks of the N. Y. C. & H. R. R. R. Company. The board of estimate and apportionment of the city of New York granted the company, on February 14, 1912, a franchise for the period of fourteen years, with the right to renew the franchise privileges for ten years at the expiration of the original term. *1916 Annual Report of the Public Service Commission for the First District*, p. 605.

New York Edison Company, the United Electric Light and Power Company, and the Long Acre Electric Light and Power Company. South of 136th street all three companies operate, although the area supplied by the Long Acre Electric Light and Power Company is confined to the nineteenth ward.[1] North of 136th street the United Electric Light and Power Company operates alone. The territory covered by the franchises owned by each of the companies exceeds the actual area of supply taken over by each of them. The old city of New York included all of what is now the borough of Manhattan and that part of the borough of The Bronx which is west of the Bronx river; and the franchises granted by the old city of New York, now held by the three companies operating in the borough of Manhattan, covered the area, "The City of New York." Certainly, the franchises held by each of the three companies entitle the owners to extend the area of supply over what was the old city of New York; and, with the annexation to the city of the territory east of the Bronx river, the franchise rights were probably automatically extended so as to include the city of New York with its enlarged territorial limits. The theory of franchise extension by annexation is not unanimously conceded to be correct; but it appears a reasonable theory. It could not, however, apply to the present city of Greater New York, since "section 1538 of chapter 378 of the Laws of 1897 (Greater New York charter) provided specifically against the territorial expansion of existing franchise rights."[2] In the borough of The

[1] The New York Edison Company furnishes direct current, and the United Electric Light and Power Company alternating current. In the streets where both companies have mains, the competition is often very vigorous. The New York Edison Company does furnish alternating current, as well, but not the alternating current suited for lighting purposes.

[2] Maltbie, *Franchises of Electrical Corporations*, p. 15.

Bronx, three companies operate: the New York Edison Company, the Bronx Gas and Electric Company, and the Westchester Lighting Company. The New York Edison Company furnishes electric lighting in that part of The Bronx which is west of the Bronx river. East of the Bronx river, in what used to be the old town of Westchester, exclusive of the incorporated village of Williamsbridge, the operating company is the Bronx Gas and Electric Company; and in the remaining area of The Bronx east of the Bronx river, electric lighting is carried on by the Westchester Lighting Company. In the first four wards of the borough of Queens, the New York and Queens Electric Light and Power Company supplies electricity;[1] in the fifth ward of the borough of Queens, the Queens Borough Gas and Electric Company.

With the exception of the twenty-ninth ward of the borough of Brooklyn, and Ocean Parkway from Foster Avenue to the Atlantic ocean, territories given over to the Flatbush Gas Company, the Brooklyn Edison Company, Inc. has a monopoly of the electric business in the borough of Brooklyn. In the borough of Richmond, the Richmond Light and Railroad Company supplies electric current.

On May 21, 1901, the New York Edison Company was formed by a consolidation of the Edison Electric Illuminating Company of New York and the New York Gas and Electric Light, Heat and Power Company. On December 17, 1880, the Edison Electric Illuminating Company of New York had merged into itself the Harlem Lighting Company

[1] Another company filing certain data with the public service commission for the first district is the Bowery Bay Electric Light and Power Company. This company has no franchise. It operates during the summer months only, when it supplies electric current to the tenants at the private summer resort of North Beach, in the borough of Queens, ward 2. *1916 Annual Report of the Public Service Commission*, pp. 353, 496.

and the Manhattan Electric Light Company. The Manhattan Electric Light Company was a consolidation of the Manhattan Electric Light Company, Limited, and the Madison Square Light Company. The Madison Square Light Company was a reorganization of the Thomas-Houston Electric Company (previously known as the East River Electric Light Company). The New York Gas and Electric Light, Heat and Power Company had, on February 1, 1900, absorbed by merger six companies: the Mount Morris Electric Light Company, the North River Electric Light and Power Company, the Borough of Manhattan Electric Company, the New York Heat, Light and Power Company, the Manhattan Lighting Company, and the Block Lighting and Power Company No. 1. The North River Electric Light and Power Company was a reorganization of the North New York Lighting Company. The New York Heat, Light and Power Company had been incorporated as a consolidation of the New York Heat, Light and Power Company and the Excelsior Steam Power Company.[1] According to the last annual report of the public service commission for the first district of the state of New York to the legislature, the Consolidated Gas Company of New York is recorded as holding 602,918 out of 659,534 shares of the New York Edison Company, and is reported as owning 56,516 additional shares that represent certificates not in its own name.[2]

The United Electric Light and Power Company was incorporated on February 3, 1887, under the name of "The Safety Electric Light and Power Company." The company's name was changed to the present form on November

[1] Maltbie, *Franchises of Electrical Corporations in Greater New York*, pp. 44-5.

[2] Public Service Commission, First District, *Annual Report for 1916*, p. 520.

8, 1889. It has acquired control through stock ownership of the Ball Electrical Illuminating Company and the Brush Electric Illuminating Company of New York, two dormant companies. It absorbed by merger the United States Illuminating Company. According to the report of the commission the Consolidated Gas Company of New York is recorded as holding 51,139 out of 53,180 outstanding shares of the United Electric Light and Power Company, and is reported as owning 1,819 additional shares that represent certificates not in its own name.[1] The Brush Electric Illuminating Company of New York retains ownership of its franchise, as does the Ball Electrical Illuminating Company. The New York Edison Company took over the plant of the Brush Electric Illuminating Company of New York, and, in accordance with an agreement renewed for ten years from May 1, 1914, continues to supply the former consumers of the Brush Company with electric current.

The Long Acre Electric Light and Power Company was incorporated on April 24, 1903. The franchise under which it operates was originally granted to the American Electric Manufacturing Company, passed by various transfers to Martin Minturn, who sold it on March 21, 1906, to the Long Acre Electric Light and Power Company. Although the company conducts but limited operations, its franchise territory legally extends throughout the borough of Manhattan and at least that part of the borough of The Bronx which is west of the Bronx river. As its name implies, the Bronx Gas and Electric Company supplies both gas and electricity. It was incorporated on August 16, 1893. The Westchester Lighting Company, incorporated on November 5, 1900, operates both within the city of New York and outside the city limits. This study is concerned with the city operations only. The corporate history of the company in-

[1] *Public Service Commission Report, 1916*, p. 617.

cludes about thirty predecessor companies.[1] Three are of interest because of their figuring as original grantees of franchises under which the Westchester Lighting Company carries on its electric lighting business in the city of New York: the Pelham Bay Park Electric Light, Power and Storage Company, the Eastchester Electric Company, and the Pelham Electric Light and Power Company. The present operating company holds all of the capital stock of the Pelham Bay Park Electric Light, Power and Storage Company, and merged into itself the Eastchester Electric Company and the Pelham Electric Light and Power Company. The Flatbush Gas Company was incorporated on April 2, 1864. It was originally incorporated as a gas-light company; but after filing an amended certificate of incorporation allowing for the manufacture and distribution of electricity, it purchased the franchise of the Knickerbocker Electric Light and Power Company. The Brooklyn Union Gas Company, which owns the capital stock of the Flatbush Gas Company,[2] furnishes to the latter company the gas it distributes.

The New York and Queens Electric Light and Power Company, incorporated on July 21, 1900, absorbed by merger the New York and Queens Gas and Electric Company, the Jamaica Electric Light Company, the Electric Illuminating and Power Company of Long Island City, and the Long Island Illuminating Company. The New York and Queens Gas and Electric Company had absorbed by merger the Newtown Light and Power Company, the New York and Queens Light and Power Company, and the Flushing Gas and Electric Light Company.[3] According to the last

[1] Maltbie, *Franchises of Electrical Corporations*, p. 67.

[2] *Public Service Commission Report*, 1916, p. 447.

[3] Maltbie, *Franchises of Electrical Corporations*, pp. 123-127.

annual report of the commission, the Consolidated Gas Company of New York is reported as having stock control of the New York and Queens Electric Light and Power Company. Out of the outstanding 12,500 shares of common stock in 1913, the Consolidated Gas Company of New York held 9,659; and out of the outstanding 12,500 shares of preferred stock, 7,612. 4,883 shares of preferred stock, and 6,683 of common stock were recorded as held by the Consolidated Gas Company of New York in 1916, together with 3,090 shares of preferred stock and 3,417 shares of common stock owned, but representing certificates not in its own name.[1]

The Queens Borough Gas and Electric Company, incorporated on May 29, 1902, absorbed by merger the Town of Hempstead Gas and Electric Company and the Queens Borough Electric Light and Power Company. The Queens Borough Electric Light and Power Company had purchased the franchises of the Citizens Lighting Company, and "certain electric lighting rights, held by Van Wyck Rossiter personally."[2] Van Wyck Rossiter was the president of the Citizens Lighting Company.

The Richmond Light and Railroad Company, as its name implies, operates both as a lighting company and an electric railroad. Its name was changed on August 18, 1902, from that of *Richmond Light Company* to the name it now bears,[3] and its corporate powers extended to include the operation of an electric railroad. The corporate history of the electricity division of the Richmond Light and Railroad Company may, for the purposes of this study, be narrowed down to those companies that were original grantees of the franchises now held by the company. The Richmond

[1] *Public Service Commission Report*, 1916, p. 496.

[2] Maltbie, *Franchises of Electrical Corporations*, p. 150.

[3] *Report of Public Service Commission*, 1916, p. 592.

County Electric Light Company sold to the New York and Staten Island Electric Company its property and franchises.[1] The Richmond Light and Railroad Company acquired, in 1902, the properties of the New York and Staten Island Electric Company, sold under foreclosure proceedings.[2]

The Brooklyn Edison Company, Inc., assumed its present name as recently as January 10, 1919, having been known formerly as the Kings County Electric Light and Power Company. Since October 30, 1899, the Edison Electric Illuminating Company of Brooklyn had operated the property of the Kings County Electric Light and Power Company. By a petition dated December 2, 1918, the latter company asked the public service commission for permission to merge into itself the Edison Electric Illuminating Company of Brooklyn and to execute a mortgage to be designated as its general mortgage upon all its plant and property; and by a petition dated December 9, 1918, it applied for an order to authorize it to issue $6,000,000 par value of the general mortgage gold bonds, series A. On January 27, 1919, the public service commission approved the merger and consented to the execution by the Brooklyn Edison Company, Inc., of a general mortgage, bearing the date of January 1, 1919, and on the same date the commission authorized the issuance of bonds to the amount of $5,500,000 face value. In giving the order to merge, the commission expressly provided that the permission of the commission should not be construed to validate any invalid franchises, or revive any expired franchises, or change any terms in any franchises, or bear upon the rights of the merged or merging company in pending litigation affecting

[1] Maltbie, *Franchises of Electrical Corporations*, p. 202.

[2] *Report of Public Service Commission*, 1916, p. 592.

them. The consent of the commission to the general mortgage was conditioned upon the preliminary merging of the Edison Electric Illuminating Company of Brooklyn into the Brooklyn Edison Company, Inc.; the consent of the stockholders of the merging company to the mortgage; the full right of the commission to determine the accuracy of statements set forth in the mortgage; and the authorization by the commission of any desired issuance of bonds by the company in pursuance of the terms of the mortgage.[1] In authorizing the issue of $5,500,000 face value of principal of bonds of the Brooklyn Edison Company, Inc., the commission stipulated that the merging of the Edison Electric Illuminating Company of Brooklyn into the petitioning company must precede any issuance of bonds; that the proceeds of the sale of bonds must net the Brooklyn Edison Company, Inc., at least eighty-five per cent of the par value of the bonds besides accrued interest on the principal, and must be used only for the following purposes: [2]

(1) To or toward reimbursement of moneys actually expended from income of said Brooklyn Edison Company, Inc., and said Edison Electric Illuminating Company of Brooklyn or from said other moneys in the treasury of said companies for acquisition of property and for extension and improvement of the facilities, plant and distributing system of said Brooklyn Edison Company, Inc., between October 1, 1912 and December 31, 1918 .... $2,325,000

(2) For the discharge or refunding of obligations of the Brooklyn Edison Company, Inc., incurred by the Edison Electric Illuminating Company of Brooklyn for the acquisition of property or for the construction, completion, extension or improvement of said facilities, plant or distributing system, de-

[1] See Order approving merger and consenting to mortgage, and Memorandum upon granting of application, case no. 2351.

[2] Order authorizing issuance of bonds, case no. 2352, pp. 3, 4.

scribed below or to any renewals thereof or substitutes therefor $2,350,000

(3) For expenses of sale of bonds hereby authorized and to make up the discount or deficiency, if any, in the amount realized from the sale to net not less than eighty-five (85) per cent. of par of the bonds sold for the purposes specified in subdivisions (1) and (2) of Section 4, and to be applied pro rata for the purposes therein stated, not exceeding the sum of $825,000

The commission further conditioned its consent to the issuance of the bonds by limiting the application of the authority to issue to bonds issued by the Brooklyn Edison Company, Inc., on or before December 31, 1919; by stipulating that the company keep full and separate accounts of the sale and disposal of the proceeds of the bonds, and subject such records to auditing by accountants selected from time to time by the commission; and by limiting the sum allowed for the expense incurred in the approval, issuance and sale of the bonds, and setting forth the details expected of the company in establishing and maintaining an amortization fund.

In the memorandum written by one of the commissioners upon the granting of the application to merge and to execute the general mortgage, attention is directed to the advantages which the merger will bring both to the companies and to the city of New York. The Edison Electric Illuminating Company of Brooklyn, the operating company, has continued to own the greater part of the distributing system in the borough of Brooklyn, even as the Kings County Electric Light and Power Company has kept ownership of the large generating system; but the business has been conducted as a unified whole. The Edison Electric Illuminating Company of Brooklyn, having leased all the property and franchises of the Kings County Electric Light and

Power Company, has been paying taxes and assessments on its own property and its leased property, as well as interest on various bonds of the Kings County Electric Light and Power Company; and has turned over its net annual profits to the Kings County Company. In order to finance the large expenditures called for by the need of additional facilities and equipment demanded by the progressively expanding business of the electric system in the borough of Brooklyn, the Kings County Electric Light and Power Company has been issuing capital stock and debenture bonds, and has taken notes from the Edison Electric Illuminating Company of Brooklyn for that part of the expenditure attributable to the property of the operating company. In commenting upon the situation, the memorandum states: [1]

The multiplication of intercorporate transactions is not only uneconomical but difficult in handling. The marketing of the bonds of the Kings County Company with the obligations of the Edison Company as security has not proven satisfactory. In order permanently to finance the large improvements and extensions, the companies have formulated a plan under which the securities issued therefor shall be a direct lien upon the physical assets and not upon the capital stock or notes. . . . . The merger will eliminate the maintenance of two separate sets of accounts and the recording and adjustment of intercompany claims. One statement will suffice to show the financial condition of all the properties owned or possessed or operated by the merged companies. It will also avoid the difficulty of allocating to the individual companies' properties the expenditures made. The securities issued will be secured directly by the property instead of by obligations, and many features of holding company entanglements will be eliminated.

[1] Kracke, *Memorandum upon granting of application to merge and execute a general mortgage*, case no. 2351, pp. 2, 3.

The memorandum referred to the objections made by the corporation counsel of the city of New York to the granting of the application to merge, and stated the city's contention

That any consent, approval or order granted by the Commission would be a recognition by the Commission of the existence of franchise rights whose validity was questioned and would prejudice the rights asserted by the city and citizens thereof in certain litigation which is pending and in which the validity of the franchise claimed and exercised by the companies was contested.[1]

Replying to these objections, the memorandum said: "By the express provisions of Section 15 of the Stock Corporations Law the merger cannot in any way change the estate, property, rights, privileges and franchises of the merged corporation."

The memorandum calls particular attention to the probable embarrassment that would ensue in the operations of the companies if they were not allowed to change their corporate form by merger so as to be able to finance successfully the expenditures of the past and the present called for by the need of serving the community. It further stated:[2]

At the hearing, it was stated by the Counsel for the companies that the City would be financially benefited by the merger. Under the franchise granted by the City of Brooklyn to the Kings County Electric Light and Power Company, which became effective June 26, 1894, the company was obligated to pay the City one per cent. of its gross receipts or revenues derived from whatsoever source for the six months preceding. Under the dual corporate organization the gross receipts of the Kings County Electric Light and Power Com-

[1] Kracke, *Memorandum upon granting application to merge*, p. 3.

[2] *Ibid.*, p. 5.

pany consisted of the moneys paid by the Edison Company to the Kings County Company after the operating expenses and taxes and other charges of the Edison Company had been paid. Upon effecting the merger, it was stated to be the intention of the new company to pay the one per cent. on the gross income of the merging company, which will be much greater than the income of the Kings County Company.

In a more appropriate connection hereafter [1] each franchise in the system of the Brooklyn Edison Company, Inc., is discussed as to the matter of transfers. This discussion completes the corporate history of the company.

Mention should be made, in passing, of the Consolidated Telegraph and Electrical Subway Company and the Empire City Subway, Limited.[2] The New York Edison Company has stock control of the Consolidated Telegraph and Electrical Subway Company, a company incorporated on December 26, 1885, for constructing and operating subways for electrical conductors in the city of New York, and owning the subways in the boroughs of Manhattan and The Bronx which are used for high-tension electric light and power purposes. The control of the Empire City Subway Company, Limited, a company incorporated on July 12, 1890, and carrying on the business of constructing and leasing subways for low-tension electrical conductors in the boroughs of Manhattan and The Bronx, has been acquired by the New York Telephone Company through majority ownership of its capital stock.

Attention may next be directed to the subject of the special franchises of the several companies.

By the enactment of chapter 712 of the laws of 1899, special franchises were made taxable property. The chapter became a law with the approval of the governor on May

[1] See ch. iv.

[2] *Report of Public Service Commission*, 1916, pp. 420, 441.

26, 1899. It was an act to amend the tax law, in relation to the taxation of public franchises as real property. Subdivision three of section two of the tax law was amended to read:

The terms *land, real estate,* and *real property,* as used in this chapter, include the land itself above and under water, all buildings and other articles and structures, substructures and superstructures, erected upon, under or above, or affixed to the same; . . . . all supports and inclosures for electrical conductors and other appurtenances upon, under, and above ground; all surface, under ground or elevated railroads, including the value of all franchises, rights or permission to construct, maintain, or operate the same in, under, above, on or through, streets, highways, or public places; . . . all mains, pipes and tanks laid or placed in, upon, above or under any public or private street or place for conducting steam, heat, water, oil, electricity or any property, substance or product capable of transportation or conveyance therein or that is protected thereby, including the value of all franchises, rights, authority or permission to construct, maintain, or operate, in, under, above, upon or through, any streets, highways, or public places, any mains, pipes, tanks, conduits, or wires, with their appurtenances, for conducting water, steam, heat, light, power, gas, oil, or other substance, or electricity for telegraphic, telephonic or other purposes . . . . A franchise, right, authority or permission specified in this subdivision shall for the purpose of taxation be known as a *special franchise.* A special franchise shall be deemed to include the value of the tangible property of a person, co-partnership, association or corporation situated in, upon, under or above any street, highway, public place or public waters in connection with the special franchise. The tangible property so included shall be taxed as a part of the special franchise.

The first assessment under the new law was made in 1900. The following table shows the assessed valuation, by boroughs, as fixed by the state board of tax commissioners, of the special franchises of the city of New York from 1900 to 1918 inclusive.[1]

ASSESSED VALUATIONS OF SPECIAL FRANCHISES FROM 1900 TO 1918

Year	*Manhattan*	*The Bronx*	*Brooklyn*
1900	$166,763,669	$7,272,249	$39,250,552
1901	160,954,387	7,466,283	35,084,220
1902	167,169,240	9,071,700	37,522,490
1903	177,447,700	9,573,100	41,124,700
1904	189,944,100	10,791,600	43,790,950
1905	228,054,000	14,117,000	52,206,950
1906	268,565,750	13,992,000	68,787,750
1907	336,346,500	21,521,000	95,311,300
1908	346,569,200	23,610,300	103,900,150
1909	334,299,800	23,209,400	98,976,500
1910	328,012,100	20,076,100	100,218,200
1911	324,651,100	27,443,600	109,940,300
1912	277,836,600	23,305,400	94,615,990
1913	297,674,923	24,741,625	98,440,849
1914	282,194,094	26,147,758	78,261,638
1915	265,340,985	25,010,258	73,017,854
1916	280,248,618	32,053,720	91,107,508
1917	302,494,867	35,939,013	94,532,547
1918	282,825,592	32,097,927	92,659,654

Year	*Queens*	*Richmond*	*Total*
1900	$4,036,817	$2,356,064	$219,679,351
1901	5,768,494	2,060,810	211,334,194
1902	5,264,900	1,591,825	220,620,155
1903	5,528,000	1,510,825	235,184,325
1904	5,496,600	1,498,200	251,521,450
1905	6,232,600	1,583,000	302,193,550
1906	8,333,300	1,800,500	361,479,300
1907	11,698,700	1,977,500	466,855,000
1908	15,902,070	2,508,750	492,490,470
1909	14,876,700	2,639,500	474,001,900
1910	14,917,800	2,185,400	465,409,600
1911	16,400,400	2,582,700	481,018,100
1912	15,031,989	2,358,780	413,148,799
1913	15,428,524	2,575,660	438,861,581

[1] *Report of Taxes and Assessments of the City of New York*, 1918, p. 24.

ASSESSED VALUATIONS OF SPECIAL FRANCHISES FROM 1900 TO 1918
(*Continued*)

Year	*Queens*	*Richmond*	*Total*
1914	15,446,039	2,370,782	404,420,311
1915	14,288,994	2,314,979	379,973,070
1916	18,786,164	3,156,652	425,352,662
1917	24,436,374	4,164,844	461,567,645
1918	27,479,195	4,411,730	439,474,098

By a search through the annual records of the department of taxes and assessments in the city of New York, figures showing the special franchise assessments of the electric-lighting companies may be obtained. The figures presented here are for the years 1915 to 1918 inclusive. The Queens Borough Gas and Electric Company and the Westchester Lighting Company operate both within and outside the city limits, but the assessed valuations given below are for New York City only. In the case of the Richmond Light and Railroad Company, the valuation of the special franchise is not divided between the electric and railroad divisions, but covers both divisions. Although a company may be operating in more than one borough, the amount shown in the table covers its special franchise assessment throughout the complete area of operation. Naturally, it is the Edison Electric Illuminating Company of Brooklyn, and not the Brooklyn Edison Company, Inc., which is listed, because it was in the year 1919 that the former company was merged into the Kings County Electric Light and Power Company, the name of which became the Brooklyn Edison Company, Inc. As has been indicated in the merger case, the Edison Electric Illuminating Company of Brooklyn, as the operating company, paid the taxes of the lessor company, the Kings County Electric Light and Power Company. The latter company, therefore, is not found in the list. The situation is different, however, with the other company in the system, the Amsterdam Electric

Light, Heat and Power Company. Although not operating, it is assessed separately. Finally, the Brush Electric Illuminating Company of New York, although not operating, comes in for its own special franchise assessment, apart from that of the United Electric Light and Power Company.

Special Franchise Valuations of Electric Lighting Companies in Assessments from 1915 to 1918

Name of Company	*Year* 1915	1916	1917	1918
New York Edison Company.	$42,795,480	$45,165,700	$62,905,400	$53,646,950
United Electric Light and Power Company.	6,956,950	9,997,500	10,105,000	7,120,000
Long Acre Electric Light and Power Company.	91,000	93,000	94,000	95,000
Bronx Gas and Electric Company.	364,000	423,200	427,800	404,550
Westchester Lighting Company.	445,900	460,000	558,000	595,200
Edison Electric Illuminating Company of Brooklyn.	12,849,200	18,292,360	19,065,000	19,270,000
Flatbush Gas Company.	1,257,620	1,271,440	2,325,000	1,880,000

SPECIAL FRANCHISE VALUATIONS OF ELECTRIC LIGHTING COMPANIES IN ASSESSMENTS FROM 1915 TO 1918 (*Continued*)

Name of Company	*Year* 1915	1916	1917	1918
New York and Queens Electric Light and Power Company.	712,000	1,677,850	4,009,700	4,405,500
Queens Borough Gas and Electric Company.	178,000	411,180	411,180	411,180
Richmond Light and Railroad Company.	578,500	890,000	1,424,000	1,424,000
Brush Electric Illuminating Company of New York.	273,000	279,000	282,000	418,000
Amsterdam Electric Light, Heat and Power Company.	54,600	74,520	102,300	103,400
Total	$66,556,250	$79,035,750	$101,709,380	$89,773,780

The table shows that the greatest valuation is placed upon the special franchises of the New York Edison Company. Next in order of importance come the Edison Electric Illuminating Company of Brooklyn and the United Electric Light and Power Company. If the year 1918 be considered exclusively, the New York Edison Company was assessed 59.7% of the total for that year; the Edison Electric Illuminating Company of Brooklyn, 21.4% and the United Electric Light and Power Company, 7.9%. Further, if the totals compiled in the table be compared with the totals for the same years in the preceding table, it appears that in 1915 the special franchise valuation of the electric-lighting companies of the city of New York was 17.5% of the total valuation of all the special franchises in the city; in 1916, 18.5%; in 1917, 22.0%; and in 1918 20.4%.

What part of the valuation placed by the state tax commission upon the special franchises of the electric-lighting companies of the city of New York, is adjudged by it to belong to the intangible element of the special franchises; *i. e.*, the right to occupy the streets? The total valuation, as is indicated by the definition of a special franchise, includes a value placed upon tangible property and a value placed upon intangible property. What is the valuation placed upon the intangible property? The state tax commissioners are not required by law to follow any definite rule in ascertaining the value of special franchises; but where they determine the value of the intangible element of the special franchise by the application of the rule of net earnings, they are following the method of capitalizing the net earnings in order to ascertain the value of the intangible right. This rule of net earnings was approved by the court of appeals in the Jamaica Water Supply case.[1] The method was to deduct from gross earnings the operating and maintenance expenses [2] and a fair return on the amount invested in tangible property used in connection with the franchise. The remainder was considered as the profits due to the exercise of the special franchise. These profits, or net earnings, were capitalized at a rate of one per cent higher than the rate allowed on the investment in the tangible property; and the result was taken as the value of the intangible

[1] Jamaica Water Supply Company *v.* Tax Commissioners, 128 N. Y. App. Div., 13.

[2] Allowance for depreciation is made.

element of the special franchise. The full value of the special franchise was obtained by adding to the capitalized net earnings the present value of the tangible, special franchise property in streets, highways, and public places. Since, however, the courts had ruled that special franchises be not assessed for the purposes of taxation at a higher percentage of value than that placed upon real estate by the local assessors, the full valuation of the special franchise was equalized. The equalized valuation has the same ratio to the full valuation as has the assessed value of local real estate to the full valuation of that real estate. The current tax rate is applied, then, to the equalized value of the special franchise.

The operation of the net-earnings rule is shown in the case of People *ex rel.* Union Railway of New York City *v.* the State Board of Tax Commissioners, although in this instance the capitalization of net earnings is at the same rate as the rate of return allowed on the tangible property:[1]

Gross revenue from fares		$1,987,343.29
Other income including		
Rent of equipment	$1,236.00	
Adv. in cars	28,650.00	
Rent of tracks	31,517.13	
Car and station privileges	49.47	
Sale of power	2,555.95	
Interest	715.76	
		64,724.31
Total gross earnings		$2,052,067.60
Less operating expenses		1,232,595.97
Net income from transportation		$819,471.63
Less taxes and other expenses		82,319.12
		$737,152.51

[1] *The New York Law Journal*, April 17, 1913.

Less 6% return on the amount of relator's entire property used in operation, including		
(1) Property in the streets	$1,636,738.89	
(2) Property outside streets	905,026.89	
(3) Real estate	418,600.00	
	$2,960,365.78	177,621.68
		$559,530.73
Less depreciation fund		151,366.18
Net earnings attributable to special franchise		$408,164.55
Latter capitalized at 6% is the value of the intangible right, or		$6,802,742.50
Add value of tangible property		1,636,738.89
		$8,439,481.39
Equalize at 90% gives		7,595,533.25

The year 1918 is selected as the period for which to determine the valuation placed by the state tax commission upon the intangible element of the special franchises under which the electric-lighting companies of the city of New York are operating. The data used herein have been obtained from the annual records of the department of taxes and assessments in the city, from reports of the electric-lighting companies to the public service commission for the first district (which contain certain data taken from the reports made by the companies to the state tax commission), and from letters from the state tax commission itself. Through the courtesy of the state tax department, there were obtained two sets of valuations covering the special franchise assessments of the ten electric-lighting companies for the year 1918, one set showing the full valuation and the other the equalized assessment. By a search through the annual records of the department of taxes and assessments for 1918, the part of the assessment falling upon the company in each of the boroughs in which it was operating was found. In the reports of the companies to the public service commission for the first district were listed the present value of the tangible property in streets, highways, and public places; in other words, the companies' estimate of the present value of the tangible element of the special franchise. In order to arrive at the valuation placed upon the intangible element of the special franchise, we subtract from the full valuation of the special franchise the present value of the tangible property in streets, highways, and public places.

While it is of interest to obtain the approximate valuation placed upon the intangible element of the special franchises under which the electric-light companies are operating, it must be emphasized that the result is only an approximation. The state tax commissioners take into account, in respect to earnings and operating expenses connected with the net-earnings rule, information frequently submitted by the companies subsequent to the date of the report made to the public service commission. This information is not included in the calculations herewith made in order to arrive at the valuation of the intangible element. Moreover, the state tax commissioners do not concede that a company is justified in reporting the same figures for cost of reproduction as for present value. Many of the companies appear to hold that the present value of the property in streets, highways, and public places is the same as the reproduction cost. The state tax commissioners arrive at the present value of the tangible property of these companies by deducting the accrued depreciation from the reported reproduction cost; and they use that present value in the net-earnings rule, both as a basis for return and as the tangible element in the special franchise valuation. Therefore, the result obtained by deducting from the full, special franchise valuation the present value of the tangible property as reported by the companies, will be less than the actual, intangible value as determined by the state tax department. The difference will be equivalent to the amount of depreciation taken by the department but not conceded by all the companies. However, the plan which has been outlined as the one to be used in ascertaining the valuation placed upon the right to occupy the streets, is correct; and we proceed to find the valuation of the intangible element of the special franchises by taking the difference between the full valuation of the special franchises and the present value, as reported by the companies, of the tangible property in streets, highways, and public places.

The 1918 special franchise valuations are based on reports of the companies to the tax commission for the year ended December 31, 1916, with property valuation as of the same date. That date was given in the records filed with the public service commission, both as to the time of report to the tax commission and the date as to which valuation was made, in the case of the United Electric Light and Power Company, the Bronx Gas and Electric Company, and the New York and Queens Electric Light and Power Company. No report was found among the records of the public service commission intervening between the two valuations of October 1, 1916, and October 1, 1917, filed by the Edison Electric Illuminating Company of Brooklyn. The valuation of the former date is selected. The New York Edison Company and the Flatbush Gas Company stated June 30, 1916, both as the date of report to the tax commission and the date as to which valuation was made; and they appear to have filed nothing further with the public service commission till the record which gives December 31, 1917, as both the date of report to the tax commission and that of valuation. The amount stated for June 30, 1916, is therefore taken. In the case of the Richmond

Light and Railroad Company and the Queens Borough Gas and Electric Company the earlier records note September 30, 1916, as the date of report to the tax commission, and June 30, 1916, as the date of valuation; and the later records indicate that a report to the tax commission was made by the Richmond Light and Railroad Company on October 15, 1917, with respect to valuation of June 30, 1917, and by the Queens Borough Gas and Electric Company on December 31, 1917, both as to the date of the report to the tax commission and the date as to which valuation was made. For both those companies the valuation of June 30, 1916, is selected. The Long Acre Electric Light and Power Company did not report any estimated values of its property for purposes of its taxation to the public service commission for the first district in the report for the year ended December 31, 1916, for the reason that in that year the commission began supplying the company with a copy of the report form used by the second district commission for class C (small) companies. This report form contains no inquiries with regard to estimated values of the company's property for purposes of taxation. However, the company did report to the public service commission in 1915, giving the estimated value of its tangible property in streets, highways, and public places, and stating June 30, 1915, as the date of report to the tax commission and as the date as to which valuation was made. Accordingly, the valuation of June 30, 1915, will be used in estimating the valuation of the intangible element of the special franchises of the company for the year 1918. By consulting the special franchise assessments of this company from 1915 to 1918 inclusive, it will be seen that no great variation is manifest. In 1915 the special franchise valuation was $91,000; in 1916, $93,000; in 1917, $94,000; and in 1918, $95,000. However, the departure from accuracy, by taking the 1915 instead of the 1916 report on which to base the special franchise valuation of 1918, is clearly indicated.

The United Electric Light and Power Company reports the same figures for cost of reproduction as for present value, namely, $3,700,000. This figure does not include the property of the Brush Electric Illuminating Company of New York. The following companies pursue the same policy: the Flatbush Gas Company, present value of property in streets, highways, and public places, $1,751,561.67; the New York and Queens Electric Light and Power Company, $2,432,661.08; and the New York Edison Company, $20,165,587. In the case of the Bronx Gas and Electric Company, the reproduction cost is not reported, and the present value is placed at $596,678. Four companies, however, evidently allow for depreciation. The Edison Electric Illuminating Company of Brooklyn reports $12,757,678 as the reproduction cost of its tangible, real property in streets, highways, and public places, and $6,378,839 as the present value. Neither amount includes the special franchise property of the Amsterdam Electric Light, Heat and Power Company, but both include that of the lessor company, the Kings County Electric Light and Power Company. The Queens Borough Gas and Electric Company lists the reproduction cost at $380,570.50, and the present value at $189,434.37. The Richmond Light and Railroad Company estimates the former at $2,038,190 and the latter at $1,306,640. In its report to the public service commission for the year ended June 30, 1916, concerning its transportation operations, the Richmond Light and Railroad Company evidently reported as the valuation of its property for purposes of taxation, not the figures rendered to the state tax commission, but certain "book value" figures as of June 30, 1916; whereas in its report to the public service commission covering its electric light, heat and power operations for the year ended December 31, 1916, it included the figures rendered to the state tax commission, the date as of which valuation was made being June 30, 1916, and the date of the report to the tax commission being September 30, 1916. The Long Acre Electric Light and Power Company records $1,331.87 as the reproduction cost, and $998.74 as present value.

The table which sets forth the special franchise valuations of the electric-lighting companies from 1915 to 1918 reveals that the New York Edison Company is listed in 1918 at $53,646,950, and the United Electric Light and Power Company at $7,120,000. The annual records at the department of taxes and assessments contain the amount attributable to the different boroughs. Thus the New York Edison Company is recorded at $47,690,000 in Manhattan, $5,928,750 in The Bronx, and $28,200 in Brooklyn; and the United Electric Light and Power Company has a special franchise valuation of $6,887,500 in Manhattan, and $232,500 in The Bronx. It must not be assumed from these figures that the first company has a general distributing system for electric lighting in the borough of Brooklyn, nor the latter company one in the borough of The Bronx. Investigation revealed that the Brooklyn assessment of the New York Edison Company was due to ownership by the company of cables on Brooklyn Bridge; and that the assessment in The Bronx with reference to the United Electric Light and Power Company was the result of the fact that in 1918 the company undertook to supply current to the New York, New Haven and Hartford Railway.

The figures of the Bronx Gas and Electric Company appear to be anomalous. The valuation of its tangible property in streets, highways, and public places which it reported to the state tax commission is $596,678, whereas the full valuation of the tangible and intangible elements, before equalization, is only $435,000. It would probably be incorrect to assume that none of this $435,000 valuation is applicable to the intangible element. The company has endeavored to have its gas rate increased from $1.00 to $1.50 per 1000 cubic feet of gas. For the calendar year 1916, it reported to the public service commission, as the gas operating income applicable to corporate property, $45,952.50; and for the calendar year 1917, it reported only $8,188.98 (the original figure subsequently corrected to an amount several hundred dollars less). It would appear under the circumstances that in any valuations reported by itself, it might be expected to report figures that would at least equal cost or book value in order to have the size of the rate base as large as possible. On the other hand, if the above $8,188.98, or the corrected figure, really fairly represents the income applicable to its total gas-property investment, than the valuation of the company's tangible gas property in streets, highways, and public places, after proper allowance has been made for the real estate outside of streets when such valuation is based on income, may very properly be taken at a figure much less than its cost or book value.

Although the Westchester Lighting Company filed certain data in 1916 with the public service commission for the first district regarding its operations in the city of New York, it appears not to have recorded the present value of its tangible property in streets, highways, and public places in the city. The company is listed in the last annual report of the public service commission as a second district company. Consequently, the figures representing the separate valuation of the tangible and the intangible part of the special franchises in the totals in the table, are exclusive of the Westchester Lighting Company.

It has been pointed out that the special franchise valuations listed in the annual records of the department of taxes and assessments represent equalized, not full, valuations. The official equalization ratios for the counties comprising the city of New York, for the years 1914 to 1917 inclusive, are given in the table below.[1]

	1914	*1915*	*1916*	*1917*
New York	91	93	94	94
Bronx	91	92	93	93
Kings	91	92	93	93
Queens	89	89	89	89
Richmond	89	89	89	89

The table will now be shown which sums up the long analysis regarding the valuation placed upon the intangible element or part of the special franchises of the ten operating companies of the city of New York. Through the courtesy of the state tax commission, figures showing the exact, full valuation of the special franchises were obtained.

VALUATION OF INTANGIBLE ELEMENT OF SPECIAL FRANCHISES OF ELECTRIC LIGHTING COMPANIES OF NEW YORK CITY IN 1918

Companies	*Equalized valuation of special franchise*	*Full valuation of special franchise*	*Valuation of tangible part of special franchise*	*Valuation of intangible part of special franchise*
New York Edison Co.	$53,646,950	$56,605,000	$20,165,587	$36,439,413
Edison Electric Illuminating Company of Brooklyn	19,270,000	20,500,000	6,378,839	14,121,161

[1] *Report of the Mayor's Advisory Commission on Administration of the Tax Law*, submitted December 20, 1917, p. 5.

VALUATION OF INTANGIBLE ELEMENT OF SPECIAL FRANCHISES OF ELECTRIC LIGHTING COMPANIES OF NEW YORK CITY IN 1918 (*Concluded*)

Companies	*Equalized valuation of special franchise*	*Full valuation of special franchise*	*Valuation of tangible part of special franchise*	*Valuation of intangible part of special franchise*
United Electric Light and Power Co. ...	7,120,000	7,500,000	3,700,000	3,800,000
New York and Queens Electric Light and Power Co. ...	4,405,000	4,950,000	2,432,661.08	2,517,338.92
Flatbush Gas Co.	1,880,000	2,000,000	1,751,561.67	248,438.33
Richmond Light and Railroad Co.	1,424,000	1,600,000	1,306,640	293,360
Queens Borough Gas and Electric Co.	411,180	462,000	189,434.37	272,565.63
Long Acre Electric Light and Power Co. ...	95,000	100,000	998.74	99,001.26
Bronx Gas and Electric Co.	404,550	435,000	596,678	—161,678
Westchester Lighting Co.	595,200	640,000		
Total	$89,251,880	$94,792,000	$36,522,399.86	$57,629,600.14

The sum total of the full valuation of all the special franchises of the companies, after a deduction of the amount attributable to the Westchester Lighting Company, is $94,-152,000. It is apparent that the valuation of the intangible part of the special franchises of the companies, again exclusive of the Westchester Lighting Company, is 61.2 per cent of their full valuation. This percentage, however, derived from totals hides the real significance of the part played by the intangible right to occupy the streets. Each company, therefore, is discussed separately.

The valuation of the intangible part of the special franchises of the New York Edison Company amounts to 64.3 per cent of the full valuation of these franchises. The United Electric Light and Power Company, another company operating in the borough of Manhattan, appears to have a considerably smaller valuation placed upon the intangible right to occupy the streets. The valuation of the intangible element of its special franchises is 50.6 per cent of the full valuation. Indicative of the importance of a right to operate in the borough of Manhattan are the figures showing the relation between the valuation of the tangible property owned by the Long Acre Electric Light and Power Company in streets, highways, and public places and the intangible right to maintain and use that property. The valuation of the intangible part of the special franchise of the Long Acre Company is 99.0 per cent of the full valuation; and is intelligible in the light of the fact that it represents the enormously valuable privilege of occupying streets in the important borough of Manhattan. The New York and Queens Electric Light and Power Company and the Queens Borough Gas and Electric Company are fairly evenly matched in the relation each holds between the tangible property in the streets and the intangible right of occupation. The former's valuation of the intangible part of the special franchises amounts to 50.8 per cent of the full valuation of these grants, and the latter's, to 58.9 per cent. A marked fall in importance of the right to occupy the streets is manifested by the Flatbush Gas Company and the Richmond Light and Railroad Company. The valuation of the intangible part of the special franchises of the Flatbush Gas Company is but 12.4 per cent of the full valuation of its franchises, and, in the case of the Richmond Light and Railroad Company, only 18.3 per cent. If the figures of the table with reference to the Bronx Gas and Electric Company be accepted, it is apparent that a franchise may become a liability instead of an asset arising out of particular privileges — a liability amounting in this instance to 37.1 per cent of the full valuation of the special franchises. Finally, the valuation of the intangible element of the special franchises of the Edison Electric Illuminating Company of Brooklyn (now merged into the Brooklyn Edison Company, Inc.) is 68.8 per cent of the full valuation of these franchises.

Even after taking into consideration the qualifications which were pointed out in the beginning of this analysis of the special franchises of the companies, we observe the widest possible range in the valuations placed upon the intangible rights to occupy the streets, namely, valuations extending from below zero to ninety-nine per cent of the full valuation of the special franchises. It is not, however, a simple matter to determine what is the actual value of the tangible property in streets, highways, and public places. How much of the value of the tangible property is, after all, due to the connection this property has with the intangible right, may be ascertained, with a fair degree of accuracy, from quite another point of view; in other words, if a company lost the intangible right to occupy the streets, the value of its tangible property in streets, highways, and public places would not be more than the value it had as scrap iron or discarded appliances in general. How much of the valuation placed upon the tangible property of a company operating as a going concern under legal franchises is due to the central fact that it is being so used is not a matter of simple addition or subtraction. Finally, the instance of the Bronx Gas and Electric Company makes concrete the fluctuating character of the value of the intangible element of the special franchise, and raises the interesting point that the net earnings of a company are but one way of attempting to determine the value of the intangible right itself; and that even if that right, in the hands of a specific corporation, sinks in importance for some year or series of years, it must, after all, be judged partly by its potentialities.

CHAPTER II

Franchises Claimed by Operating Companies

On the twenty-eighth of December, 1910, Mr. Milo R. Maltbie, then a member of the public service commission for the first district, submitted to the commission a report on the franchises of electrical corporations in the city of New York.[1] The report was based upon an examination of documents in possession of the companies themselves or on file in the offices of the city, the county and the state. Mr. Delos F. Wilcox, then chief of the franchise bureau of the public service commission, analyzed the franchises concerning which the report was made.

For a background for the present study, a condensed analysis of this report is given. This chapter deals with those franchises held or claimed by the present operating electric-light companies of the city of New York. The report followed the plan of tabulating, at the close of each enumeration of franchises claimed by the companies, the chief provisions of the franchises. These tables are incorporated in part in this chapter. The explanation or elaboration of the contents of the parts incorporated is confined to outstanding points of interest, such as grounds for maintaining that the status of a franchise is in doubt, history of transfers of a franchise, or other factors of importance. The conclusions reached in the elaborate report of 1910 were reached only after investigation of painstaking

[1] Maltbie, *Franchises of Electrical Corporations in Greater New York*, a report submitted to the public service commission for the first district, December 28, 1910.

thoroughness, but the preface of the report itself bears witness to the difficulties of the task:

The investigation was thoroughly and carefully made, but there are still several points which neither the companies nor the experts of the Franchise Bureau of the Commission have been able to clarify. It may be that if the uncertainty surrounding these matters were entirely removed, certain statements in this report would need modification, but it is believed to be as accurate as can be made from the records in the files of the Commission.

For the sake of clearness, in spite of the brevity necessitated by condensing the lengthy report of 1910, the plan is here being followed of prefacing each table by an enumeration of the old political subdivisions granting the franchises tabulated, and of the several franchises granted by each. The enumeration follows the wording and order of the table of contents of the report itself, with the important exception that under each heading only those franchises are selected which are found in the tables. The remaining franchises are considered in the succeeding chapter. Reversing the order of the Report, Exhibit I is herewith given as an appropriate preliminary survey.

Population and Area of Electric Light Franchise Divisions of Greater New York[1]

Old Name of Political Subdivisions.	*Area in square miles within present city limits.*	*Population in 1910.*	*Present operating companies owning, controlling or claiming franchise rights.*
City of New York (prior to June 5, 1895).	41.40	2,713,369	New York Edison Company, United Electric Light and Power Company, Long Acre Electric Light and Power Company.

[1] Maltbie, *Franchises of Electrical Corporations*, pp. 216-217.

POPULATION AND AREA OF ELECTRIC LIGHT FRANCHISE DIVISIONS OF GREATER NEW YORK (*Continued*)

Old Name of Political Subdivisions.	*Area in square miles within present city limits.*	*Population in 1910.*	*Present operating companies owning, controlling or claiming franchise rights.*
Town of Westchester (excluding village of Williamsbridge).	13.20	31,958	Bronx Gas and Electric Company.
Village of Williamsbridge.	1.20	9,750	Westchester Lighting Company.
Village of South Mount Vernon (or Wakefield).	1.25	4,440	"
Village of Eastchester.	1.10	500	"
Town of Pelham.	3.20	2,467	"
City of Brooklyn (excluding New Utrecht and Flatlands).	47.20	1,539,823	Edison Electric Illuminating Company of Brooklyn.
City of Brooklyn.	77.60	1,634,351	Edison Electric Illuminating Co. of Brooklyn (through control of Amsterdam Electric Light and Power Co.).
Town of Flatbush (included in territory of Edison Electric Illuminating Company of Brooklyn).	5.90	73,047	Flatbush Gas Company.
City of Long Island City.	7.30	61,763	New York and Queens Electric Light and Power Co.

POPULATION AND AREA OF ELECTRIC LIGHT FRANCHISE DIVISIONS OF GREATER NEW YORK (*Continued*)

Old Name of Political Subdivisions.	*Area in square miles within present city limits.*	*Population in 1910.*	*Present operating companies owning, controlling or claiming franchise rights.*
Town of Newtown.	23.00	105,219	New York and Queens Electric Light and Power Company.
Town of Flushing (excluding villages of Flushing, Whitestone and College Point).	28.80	9,212	"
Village of Flushing.	1.65	15,366	"
Village of Whitestone.	2.10	4,000	"
Village of College Point.	1.90	8,563	"
Town of Jamaica (excluding villages of Jamaica and Richmond Hill).	52.70	37,245	"
Village of Richmond Hill (franchise for Broadway only).	1.00	12,676	"
Village of Jamaica (no franchise).	3.50	17,491	"
Town of Hempstead (portion within city limits, excluding village of Far Rockaway).	5.40	7,589	Queens Borough Gas and Electric Company.

POPULATION AND AREA OF ELECTRIC LIGHT FRANCHISE DIVISIONS OF GREATER NEW YORK (*Concluded*)

Old Name of Political Subdivisions.	*Area in square miles within present city limits.*	*Population in 1910.*	*Present operating companies owning, controlling or claiming franchise rights.*
Village of Far Rockaway.	2.30	4,887	Queens Borough Gas and Electric Company.
Village of Rockaway Beach (included in Town of Hempstead).	....	.....	"
Village of New Brighton. (Town of Castleton).	5.20	27,201	Richmond Light and Railroad Company.
Village of Port Richmond.	.90	12,701	"
Town of Northfield (excluding village of Port Richmond).	15.00	7,111	"
Village of Edgewater.	3.70	21,609	"
Town of Middletown (outside of village of Edgewater. No franchise).	5.00	1,929	"
Town of Southfield (outside of village of Edgewater).	10.50	3,995	"
Village of Tottenville.	1.10	3,568	"
Town of Westfield (excluding village of Tottenville).	15.90	7,855	"

Concerning the areas given in the above table, the Report states: [1]

In the above summary areas are included in some cases where the companies' franchise rights are doubtful, while areas are excluded where the companies have no claim to franchises except through the automatic operation of territorial expansion of the political subdivisions from which the franchises were originally acquired.

The city of New York, prior to June, 1895, included the area now embraced in the borough of Manhattan and that part of the borough of The Bronx which is west of the Bronx river. Among the franchises granted by the old city of New York were the original Edison franchise, the Brush franchise, the United States franchise, the East river franchise, and the omnibus electric franchise. The omnibus electric franchise included a franchise granted to six different companies by one resolution. Of these six, this chapter is concerned with the five franchises that were granted respectively to the American Electric Manufacturing Company, the Ball Electrical Illuminating Company, the Mount Morris Electric Light Company, the Harlem Lighting Company, and the North New York Lighting Company. The provisions of these are presented in a condensed form in tables. The original Edison franchise was granted to the Edison Electric Illuminating Company of New York; the East river franchise to the East River Electric Light Company; the United States franchise to the United States Illuminating Company of New York; and the Brush franchise to the Brush Electric Illuminating Company of New York.

[1] Maltbie, *Franchises of Electrical Corporations*, p. 217.

TABLE I [1]—ANALYSIS OF ELECTRIC LIGHT FRANCHISES HELD BY THE NEW YORK EDISON COMPANY [2]

Territory covered: Manhattan and The Bronx west of Bronx River

Original grantee.	Edison Electric Illuminating Company of New York.	East River Electric Light Company.	Harlem Lighting Co., North New York Lighting Co., and Mount Morris Electric Light Company.
Local authority.	Board of Aldermen.	Board of Aldermen.	Board of Aldermen.
Date of Franchise.	First passed March 22, 1881. Passed over veto, April 19, 1881.	Passed March 29, 1887.	Passed May 31, 1887.
Scope of franchise.	Purposes of illumination.	Electrical purposes.	Electrical purposes.
Compensation in money.	One cent per lineal foot of streets opened for underground work.	One cent per lineal foot of streets opened for other than arc lights.	One cent per lineal foot of streets opened for other than arc lights.
Grant exclusive.			No.
Grantee's "successors or assigns" recognized in franchise.	No.	Yes.	No.
Number of times franchise has been transferred.	One.	Five.	Two; three; two.

In the second table there are listed the franchises held by two of the present operating electric light companies: the

[1] Maltbie, *Franchises of Electrical Corporations*, p. 54. The table is here presented in part only.

[2] All these franchises are without time limit.

United Electric Light and Power Company, and the Long Acre Electric Light and Power Company. The franchise held by the Long Acre Electric Light and Power Company is the one granted by the board of aldermen to the American Electric Manufacturing Company by the resolutions granting the omnibus electric franchise.

TABLE II—ANALYSIS OF ELECTRIC LIGHT FRANCHISES HELD BY THE UNITED ELECTRIC LIGHT AND POWER COMPANY AND THE LONG ACRE ELECTRIC LIGHT AND POWER COMPANY[1]

Territory covered: Manhattan and The Bronx west of Bronx River

Original grantee.	United States Illuminating Company of New York.	Brush Electrical Illuminating Company of New York.	Ball Electrical Illuminating Company.	American Electric Manufacturing Company.
Local authority.	Board of Aldermen.	Board of Aldermen.	Board of Aldermen.	Board of Aldermen.
Date of franchise.	First passed April 12, 1881. Passed over veto, May 3, 1881.	First passed April 12, 1881. Passed over veto, May 3, 1881.	Passed May 31, 1887.	Passed May 31, 1887.
Scope of franchise.	Purposes of illumination.	Electricity.	Electrical purposes.	Electrical purposes.
Compensation in money.	One cent per lineal foot of streets opened for underground work.	One cent per lineal foot of streets opened for underground work.	One cent per lineal foot of streets opened for other than arc lights.	One cent per lineal foot of streets opened for other than arc lights.
Grant exclusive.			No.	No.
Grantee's "successors or assigns" recognized in franchise.	No.	No.	No.	No.

[1] Maltbie, *Franchises of Electrical Corporations*, p. 60. The table is here presented in part only.

TABLE II—ANALYSIS OF ELECTRIC LIGHT FRANCHISES HELD BY THE UNITED ELECTRIC LIGHT AND POWER COMPANY AND THE LONG ACRE ELECTRIC LIGHT AND POWER COMPANY [1] (*Concluded*)

Territory covered: Manhattan and The Bronx west of Bronx River

Number of times franchise has been transferred.	One.	One.	One.	Four.

Although the franchises granted to the Brush Electric Illuminating Company of New York and to the Ball Electrical Illuminating Company are tabulated under the caption of franchises *held* by the United Electric Light and Power Company, they are not franchises under which the United Electric Light and Power Company are entitled to operate. The Ball Electrical Illuminating Company and the Brush Electric Illuminating Company of New York, though dormant, and though controlled through stock ownership by the United Electric Light and Power Company, retain ownership of their franchises. The operating company is entitled to operate under the franchise originally granted to the United States Illuminating Company of New York, a company merged into the United Electric Light and Power Company, June 12, 1902. The one franchise of the Long Acre Electric Light and Power Company covers the same territory as that covered by the franchises of the New York Edison Company or that of the United Electric Light and Power Company. The franchise passed through four seccessive transfers: from the American Electric Manufacturing Company to Frederick E. Townsend, to the American Electric Illuminating Company, to Martin Minturn, and finally to the Long Acre Electric Light and Power Company.

[1] All these franchises are without time limit.

The old political subdivisions granting the franchises now held by the Bronx Gas and Electric Company and the Westchester Lighting Company in its operations in the First District, made up the territory now included in that part of the borough of The Bronx which is east of the Bronx river. They comprised the towns of Westchester (excluding the village of Williamsbridge), the villages of Williamsbridge, South Mount Vernon (or Wakefield), and Eastchester, and the town of Pelham. Accordingly, the table of franchises held or controlled by the Bronx Gas and Electric Company and the Westchester Lighting Company within the First District contains the franchise granted by the town of Westchester, the Williamsbridge franchises, the South Mount Vernon franchise, the Eastchester franchise, and three Pelham franchises, namely, the grant of August 22, 1890, the grant of October 9, 1893, and the grant of February 6, 1897. The one franchise belonging to the Bronx Gas and Electric Company is the grant given to the company itself, as original grantee, by the town board and highway commissioners of the town of Westchester, on September 11, 1893.

TABLE III—ANALYSIS OF ELECTRIC LIGHT FRANCHISES HELD OR CONTROLLED BY THE BRONX GAS AND ELECTRIC COMPANY AND THE WESTCHESTER LIGHTING COMPANY FOR DISTRICTS WITHIN THE LIMITS OF GREATER NEW YORK [1]

Original grantee.	Pelham Bay Park Electric Light, Power and Storage Co.	Eastchester Electric Co.	Eastchester Electric Co.[2]	Eastchester Electric Co.
Local authority.	Highway commissioners.	Board of Village Trustees.	Board of Village Trustees.	Board of Village Trustees.

[1] Maltbie, *Franchises of Electrical Corporations*, pp. 72-73. Table is contracted.

[2] "This grant was in the form of a contract executed by the parties primarily for public lighting." Maltbie, *Franchises of Electrical Corporations*, p. 73.

TABLE III—ANALYSIS OF ELECTRIC LIGHT FRANCHISES HELD OR CONTROLLED BY THE BRONX GAS AND ELECTRIC COMPANY AND THE WESTCHESTER LIGHTING COMPANY FOR DISTRICTS WITHIN THE LIMITS OF GREATER NEW YORK (*Continued*)

Date of franchise.	August 22, 1890.	December 23, 1891.	December 30, 1891.	November 26, 1892.
Territory covered.	Town of Pelham (part since annexed to New York City).	Village of Williamsbridge.	Village of Williamsbridge.	Village of South Mount Vernon (or Wakefield).
Duration of franchise.			Five years.	
Scope of franchise.	Poles and wires.	Electricity.	Electricity.	Electric lights.
Grant exclusive.			Yes.	
Grantee's "successors or assigns" recognized in franchise.	No.	No.	Yes.	No.
Number of times franchise has been transferred.	None; controlled through stock ownership.	Three.	Three.	Three.
Original grantee.	Pelham Bay Park Electric Light, Power and Storage Co.	Eastchester Electric Co.	Pelham Electric Light and Power Co.	Bronx Gas and Electric Co.
Local authority.	Department of Public Parks.	Board of Village Trustees.	Board of Parks.	Town Board and Highway Commissioners.

TABLE III—ANALYSIS OF ELECTRIC LIGHT FRANCHISES HELD OR CONTROLLED BY THE BRONX GAS AND ELECTRIC COMPANY AND THE WESTCHESTER LIGHTING COMPANY FOR DISTRICTS WITHIN THE LIMITS OF GREATER NEW YORK (*Concluded*)

Date of franchise.	Permit, October 9, 1893, authorized August 2, 1893.	May 28, 1895.	February 6, 1897.	September 11, 1893.
Territory covered.	Roads in Pelham Bay Park.	Village of Eastchester.	Roads in Pelham Bay Park.	Town of Westchester except village of Williamsbridge.
Duration of franchise.	Subject to revocation at any time.	Five years (?).		
Scope of franchise.	Light and telegraph poles.	Electricity for lighting and power.	Poles and wires.	Electricity.
Grant exclusive.		Yes.		
Grantee's "successors or assigns" recognized in franchise.	No.	No.	No.	No.
Number of times franchise has been transferred.	Four.	Three.	Three.	None.

The next table deals with an analysis of electric light franchises held by the Edison Electric Illuminating Company of Brooklyn and the Flatbush Gas Company. It must be remembered that in January, 1919, the Edison Electric

Illuminating Company of Brooklyn was merged into the Kings County Electric Light and Power Company, the new name being the Brooklyn Edison Company, Inc. Since the franchises in the system of the former Edison Electric Illuminating Company of Brooklyn have been the center of a storm of controversy during recent years and are still in dispute, a full discussion of the history of each franchise is given in the fourth chapter of this study. At this point all that needs to be presented is a condensed account of the provisions of the franchises. Among the franchises tabulated as to main provisions is the one originally granted to the Knickerbocker Electric Light and Power Company by the town board of the town of Flatbush and now owned by the Flatbush Gas Company. The former city of Brooklyn granted the so-called combination franchise, the Edison franchise, the Kings County franchise, and the State franchise. The combination franchise comprised a grant to Charles Cooper and Company, and one to Pope, Sewall and Company. The Edison franchise was granted to the Edison Electric Illuminating Company of Brooklyn; the Kings County franchise to the Kings County Electric Light and Power Company; and the State franchise to the State Electric Light and Power Company.

TABLE IV [1]—ANALYSIS OF ELECTRIC LIGHT FRANCHISES HELD BY THE EDISON ELECTRIC ILLUMINATING COMPANY OF BROOKLYN AND THE FLATBUSH GAS COMPANY [2]

Original grantee.	Pope, Sewall & Co.	Charles Cooper & Co.	Edison Electric Illuminating Co. of Brooklyn.
Local authority.	Common Council.	Common Council.	Common Council.

[1] Maltbie, *Franchises of Electrical Corporations*, pp. 92-95. The table is here presented only in part.

[2] "NOTE: In addition to its franchise secured from the old town of Flatbush,

TABLE IV—ANALYSIS OF ELECTRIC LIGHT FRANCHISES HELD BY THE EDISON ELECTRIC ILLUMINATING COMPANY OF BROOKLYN AND THE FLATBUSH GAS COMPANY [1] (*Continued*)

Date of franchise.	Passed May 12, 1884.	Passed May 12, 1884.	Passed Oct. 29, 1888.
Territory covered by franchise.	Wards 1 to 12, 20 to 25, city of Brooklyn.	Wards 13 to 19, and 27 and 28, city of Brooklyn.	Wards 1 to 28, city of Brooklyn.
Scope of franchise.	Electric lighting.	Electric lighting.	Electric lighting, electricity, or electrical currents for purposes of illumination or power.
Exclusiveness of grant, and forfeiture.	Not permanently exclusive.	Not permanently exclusive.	
Grantee's "successors or assigns" recognized in franchise.	Yes.	Yes.	Yes.
Number of times franchise has been transferred.	Two.	Two.	
Original grantee.	Kings County Electric Light and Power Company.	State Electric Light and Power Company.	Knickerbocker Electric Light and Power Company.

the Flatbush Gas Company secured a franchise from the City of New York under date of Dec. 28, 1909, by which the company is authorized to supply electricity through a narrow district extending on either side of Ocean Parkway from Foster Avenue to the Atlantic Ocean, and this grant is subject to the elaborate terms and conditions imposed by the standard form of franchises now used by the city under the provisions of the Greater New York Charter. The details of this grant are too numerous and complex to be shown in this table."—Maltbie, *Franchises of Electrical Corporations*, p. 93.

[1] See note 2, p. 64.

TABLE IV—ANALYSIS OF ELECTRIC LIGHT FRANCHISES HELD BY THE EDISON ELECTRIC ILLUMINATING COMPANY OF BROOKLYN AND THE FLATBUSH GAS COMPANY[1] (*Concluded*)

Local authority.	Common Council.	Common Council.	Town Board.
Date of franchise.	Passed June 11, 1894.	Passed over veto Dec. 30, 1895.	July 21, 1893.
Territory covered by franchise.	Wards 1 to 29, and 31, city of Brooklyn.	Wards 1 to 31, city of Brooklyn (possibly also Ward 32).	Town of Flatbush, (Ward 29) city of Brooklyn.
Scope of franchise.	Electricity for power, heat and light.	Electricity for light, heat and power.	Electricity for "lighting and using of it for power and traction."
Grantee's "successors and assigns" recognized in franchise.	Yes.	Yes.	No.
Number of times franchise has been transferred.	One.	One.	One.

The old political subdivisions that granted franchises covering the territory now occupied by the New York and Queens Electric Light and Power Company, the first four wards in the borough of Queens, were nine in number: Long Island city, the towns of Newtown, Jamaica, and Flushing, and the villages of Flushing, Whitestone, College Point, Jamaica, and Richmond Hill. The Long Island City franchise, granted to the Electric Illuminating and Power Company of Long Island City, extends over what is now the first ward of the borough of Queens. The town of

[1] See note 2, p. 64.

Newtown, now the second ward of the borough of Queens, was covered by four franchises: the Seely franchise, granted by the highway commissioners to the Newtown Electric Light Company, and covering the town of Newtown; the McKenna franchise, granted by the highway commissioners to Francis McKenna, and covering the town of Newtown; the county road franchise, granted by the board of supervisors of Queens county to the Newtown Light and Power Company, and covering the old county roads in the town of Newtown; and the Miller franchise, granted by the highway commissioners to Charles Miller, and covering the town of Newtown.

What is now the third ward of the borough of Queens is covered in part and in whole by franchises granted by the old town of Flushing, outside the villages of Flushing, Whitestone and College Point, and by those villages themselves. The town of Flushing franchises are two: the commissioners of highways and town board grant, made to the Flushing Electric Light and Power Company; and the county road franchise, granted by the board of supervisors of the county of Queens to the Flushing Electric Light and Power Company, and covering the county roads in the town of Flushing as well as in the three villages of Flushing, Whitestone and College Point. The one Flushing village franchise discussed in this chapter is the grant of 1897, made by the board of trustees to the Flushing Electric Light and Power Company, and covering the old village of Flushing. The Whitestone franchise was granted by the board of trustees of the village to the Flushing Electric Light and Power Company, and covered the village of Whitestone. The College Point franchise was granted by the board of trustees of the village to the Flushing Electric Light and Power Company, and covered the entire village of College Point.

What is now the fourth ward of the borough of Queens

is supplied with electricity by operation under franchises granted by the old political subdivisions of the town of Jamaica, outside of the old villages of Jamaica and Richmond Hill. Listed as franchises granted by the town of Jamaica are the Long Island Illuminating Company franchises, one granted to the company on January 10, 1896, and the other on January 16, 1896; the Jamaica Electric Light Company franchises, one granted to the company by the highway commissioners on October 27, 1896, and the other by the town board, on November 26, 1897; and the county road franchise, granted by the board of supervisors of the county of Queens to the Jamaica Electric Light Company. The Long Island Illuminating Company franchises, and the Jamaica Electric Light Company franchises embrace the territory included in the town of Jamaica, outside of the villages of Richmond Hill and Jamaica; and the county road franchise covered the county roads of the town, also outside of the limits of the two villages. The Richmond Hill franchise was granted by the board of trustees to the Jamaica Electric Light Company. "This grant, which was acquired directly through the merger of the grantee, covers that portion of the street known as Broadway lying within the limits of the old village of Richmond Hill." The franchises granted by the village of Jamaica are not considered in this chapter.

TABLE V—ANALYSIS OF THE ELECTRIC LIGHT FRANCHISES OF THE NEW YORK AND QUEENS ELECTRIC LIGHT AND POWER COMPANY IN LONG ISLAND CITY AND NEWTOWN [1]

Original grantee.	The Newtown Electric Light Co. (a copartnership).	Francis McKenna.	Newtown Light and Power Co.	Charles Miller.	Electric Illuminating and Power Co. of Long Island City.

[1] Maltbie, *Franchises of Electrical Corporations*, p. 132. The table is here presented only in part.

TABLE V—ANALYSIS OF THE ELECTRIC LIGHT FRANCHISES OF THE NEW YORK AND QUEENS ELECTRIC LIGHT AND POWER COMPANY IN LONG ISLAND CITY AND NEWTOWN (*Concluded*)

Date of franchise.	June 12, 1891.	May 20, 1895.	March 15, 1897.	April 28, 1897.	December 13, 1894.
Local authority.	Highway commissioners.	Highway commissioners.	Board of supervisors.	Highway commissioners.	Common Council.
Territory covered.	Town of Newtown.	Town of Newtown.	County roads in town of Newtown.	Town of Newtown.	Long Island City.
Scope of franchise.	Electricity for light only.	Electricity for light, heat or power.	Electricity for light, heat and power.	Electricity for light, heat or power.	Electric lights and power.
Grantee's "successors or assigns" recognized.	No.	Yes.	Yes.	Yes.	No.
Number of times franchise has been transferred.	Eight.	Three.	Two.	Two.	One.

TABLE VI—ANALYSIS OF ELECTRIC LIGHT FRANCHISES OF THE NEW YORK AND QUEENS ELECTRIC LIGHT AND POWER COMPANY IN WARD THREE, BOROUGH OF QUEENS (FLUSHING) [1]

Original grantee.	Flushing Electric Light and Power Co.	Flushing Electric Light and Power Co.	Flushing Electric Light and Power Co.	Flushing Electric Light and Power Co.	Flushing Electric Light and Power Co.
Date of franchise.	January 18, 1897.	April 5, 1897.	April 8, 1897.	April 13, 1897.	December 29 and 30, 1897.

[1] Maltbie, *Franchises of Electrical Corporations*, pp. 133-135. Contracted table.

TABLE VI—ANALYSIS OF ELECTRIC LIGHT FRANCHISES OF THE NEW YORK AND QUEENS ELECTRIC LIGHT AND POWER COMPANY IN WARD THREE, BOROUGH OF QUEENS (FLUSHING) (*Continued*)

Local authority.	Board of Village Trustees.	Board of Village Trustees.	Board of Village Trustees.	Board of Supervisors of Queens County.	Highway Commissioners, December 29; Town Board, December 30.
Territory covered.	Village of Flushing.	Village of College Point.	Village of Whitestone.	County roads in town of Flushing, including villages.	Town of Flushing outside of incorporated villages.
Duration of franchise.		May be revoked after three months if operation has not been begun.			Twenty-six years with right to renewal for twenty-five years on fair revaluation by board of appraisers.
Scope of franchise.		Electric light and power.	Electric light and power.	Electricity for lights, heat and power.	Electricity for lights, heat and power.
Grantee's "successors or assigns" recognized.	No.	Yes.	Yes.	Yes.	Yes.
Number of times franchise has been transferred.	Three.	Three.	Three.	Three.	Three.

TABLE VII—ANALYSIS OF ELECTRIC LIGHT FRANCHISES OF THE NEW YORK AND QUEENS ELECTRIC LIGHT AND POWER COMPANY IN WARD FOUR, BOROUGH OF QUEENS (JAMAICA) [1]

Original grantee.	Jamaica Electric Light Co.	Jamaica Electric Light Co.	Jamaica Electric Light Co.	Long Island Illuminating Co.	Long Island Illuminating Co.
Date of franchise.	Oct. 27, 1896, and Nov. 26, 1897.	Dec. 8, 1896.	Dec. 7 and 14, 1896.	Jan. 10, 1896.	Jan. 16, 1896.
Local authority.	Highway commissioners, Oct. 27, 1896; town board, Nov. 26, 1897.	Board of supervisors of Queens County.	Board of village trustees, Richmond Hill.	Town Board.	Highway commissioners.
Territory covered.	Town of Jamaica, outside villages of Jamaica and Richmond Hill.	County roads in town of Jamaica, outside of villages of Jamaica and Richmond Hill.	Broadway in village of Richmond Hill.	Town of Jamaica.	Town of Jamaica outside of incorporated villages.
Duration of franchise.	45 years from date.	45 years from date.			
Scope of franchise.	Electricity for producing light, heat and power.	Electricity for the purpose of light, heat and power.	Erection of poles.	Electricity for light, heat and power.	Electricity for producing light, heat and power.
Grantee's "successors or assigns" recognized.	"Assigns" referred to in one provision.	"Assigns" referred to in one provision.	No.	No.	No.

[1] Maltbie, *Franchises of Electrical Corporations*, pp. 136-137. The table is here given only in part.

TABLE VII—ANALYSIS OF ELECTRIC LIGHT FRANCHISES OF THE NEW YORK AND QUEENS ELECTRIC LIGHT AND POWER COMPANY IN WARD FOUR, BOROUGH OF QUEENS (JAMAICA) (*Concluded*)

Number of times franchise has been transferred.	One.	One.	One.	One.	One.

By tracing the corporate history of the operating electric light companies, the history of the transfers of many of the franchises may be obtained. Certain records of transfers, however, are not to be found in that way. An interesting record is attached to the Seely franchise, granted on July 12, 1891, by the highway commissioners of the town of Newtown to the co-partnership, the Newtown Electric Light Company:

According to the claim of the New York and Queens Company, title to this franchise passed from the Newtown Electric Light Company to John A. Seely; from him to the Newtown Electric Light and Power Company; from it through Henry C. Adams, Jr., Receiver, to J. H. Warner; from him to P. J. Bennett; from him back to J. H. Warner; from him to Thomas W. Stephens (also to quiet title, directly from John A. Seely to Thomas W. Stephens); from him to the New York and Queens Gas and Electric Company; from it by merger to the New York and Queens Electric Light and Power Company.[1]

The Newtown Electric Light Company was the predecessor of the Newtown Electric Light and Power Company, the latter company being incorporated under the laws of New Jersey. As indicated in the preceding paragraph, it eventually went into the hands of a receiver. Of the power

[1] Maltbie, *Franchises of Electrical Corporations*, p. 101.

of this company to operate in the state of New York as an electric-lighting corporation, the Report states:[1]

> So far as we have been able to determine by a search among the records in the Secretary of State's office this company never filed with that official a statement of its intention to do an electric lighting business in this state, as was required by the law in the case of a foreign electrical corporation.

The McKenna franchise was transferred by McKenna to the Newtown Light and Power Company. The Miller franchise was sold by Miller to the New York and Queens Gas and Electric Company.

The old political subdivisions which granted franchises under which the Queens Borough Gas and Electric Company is operating in the fifth ward of the borough of Queens were the town of Hempstead, the village of Far Rockaway, and the village of Rockaway Beach. Reference to the table at the opening of this chapter discloses that only a portion of the town of Hempstead is within the present city limits, and, consequently, within the limits of the fifth ward of the borough of Queens. Prior to January 1, 1898, ward five of the borough of Queens was a part of the town of Hempstead, and included the villages of Far Rockaway, Arverne-by-the-Sea, and Rockaway Beach.[2] The franchises granted by the authorities of the town of Hempstead were two: the Taylor franchise and the Myers franchise. Both covered the same territory, Rockaway Beach from Norton's bridge to the western end. "The village of Rockaway Beach, having been incorporated in 1897, several years subsequent to the grant of the Taylor and Myers franchises by the town authorities of the town of Hempstead, was, of

[1] Maltbie, *Franchises of Electrical Corporations*, p. 124.

[2] *Ibid.*, p. 141.

course, subject to those grants." [1] There were two franchises granted by the village of Far Rockaway: the Rockaway Electric Light Company franchise and the Citizens Lighting Company franchise. The only franchise to be considered in this chapter as granted by the village of Rockaway Beach is the Van Wyck Rossiter franchise, covering this village.

There is still another franchise under which the Queens Borough Gas and Electric Company claims the right to operate in the fifth ward of the borough of Queens, namely, the board of supervisors' franchise. This franchise was granted to Van Wyck Rossiter by the supervisors of Queens County, and covered the county road known as the Boulevard, or specifically, that part of the county road which was within the town of Hempstead. It is apparent, therefore, that franchise-granting authority was vested in this board of county officers.

By chapter 333 of the Laws of 1893, approved April 7, 1893, the Legislature had authorized the Board of Supervisors of any county, by a majority vote, to adopt the County Road System, and thereafter designate as county roads " such portions of the public highways in such county not within an incorporated village or city as they shall deem advisable; and shall cause such designation and a copy of such county roads to be filed in the clerk's office of such county." It was provided further that " the roads so designated shall, as far as practicable, be leading market roads in such county." It was also provided that county roads should be " exclusively under the jurisdiction of the Board of Supervisors and the County Engineer of the county, and exempt from the jurisdiction of the highway officers of the town." This provision was amended by chapter 375 of the Laws of 1895, in effect April 23, 1895, so as to permit the supervisors to designate as county roads public highways with-

[1] Maltbie, *Franchises of Electrical Corporations*, p. 147.

in the limits of incorporated villages. Village highways so designated were to be exempt from the jurisdiction of the village officers performing the duties of highway commissioners.[1]

TABLE VIII—ANALYSIS OF THE ELECTRIC LIGHT FRANCHISES CLAIMED OR HELD BY QUEENS BOROUGH GAS AND ELECTRIC COMPANY[2]

Original grantee.	James R. Taylor.	Samuel R. Myers.	Rockaway Electric Light Co.
Local authority.	Board of town auditors and highway commissioners, town of Hempstead.	Town authorities, including highway commissioners, town of Hempstead.	Village trustees, subject to approval by president of village before going into effect.
Date of franchise.	November 21, 1887.	May 2, 1889.	May 12, 1891.
Territory covered by franchise.	Rockaway Beach from Norton's Bridge to western end.	Rockaway Beach from Norton's Bridge to western end.	Village of Far Rockaway.
Scope of franchise.	Electricity for lighting.	Electricity for lighting.	Electric light (motive power on public streets excluded).
Grantee's "successors or assigns" recognized in franchise.	Yes.	Yes.	No.
Number of times franchise has been transferred.	Four (?)	Four (?)	Three (?)
Original grantee.	Citizens Lighting Company.	Van Wyck Rossiter.	Van Wyck Rossiter.
Local authority.	Village trustees.	Village trustees.	Board of Supervisors of Queens County.

[1] Maltbie, *Franchises of Electrical Corporations*, p. 103.

[2] *Ibid.*, pp. 156-159. The table is here presented in part only.

TABLE VIII—ANALYSIS OF THE ELECTRIC LIGHT FRANCHISES CLAIMED OR HELD BY THE QUEENS BOROUGH GAS AND ELECTRIC COMPANY (*Concluded*)

Date of franchise.	April 6, 1892. Amended later.	August 31, 1897.	September 28, 1897.
Territory covered by franchise.	Village of Far Rockaway.	Village of Rockaway Beach.	The Boulevard (in town of Hempstead, now in Ward 5, Borough of Queens).
Scope of franchise.	Electricity for lighting, not including motive power in any streets, (afterwards amended —date not given— so as to include light, heat and power, but not to authorize the " laying of street railroad tracks").	Electric lights and power for stationary motors, " and for no other purpose."	Electric light and power.
Grant exclusive.		No.	
Grantee's " successors or assigns " recognized in franchise.	No.	Yes.	Yes.
Number of times franchise has been transferred.	Two.	Two.	Two.

Before taking up the rights of the Queens Borough Gas and Electric Company under the six franchises analyzed in the table, attention is directed to the connection between the areas included in the old franchise-granting districts and the present fifth ward of the borough of Queens. The

Myers franchise and the Taylor franchise, as has been said, covered the same territory. The Taylor franchise covers all that part of the Fifth Ward of the borough of Queens not formerly included within the limits of the village of Far Rockaway, and the village of Far Rockaway comprised the eastern portion of the present Fifth Ward of the borough of Queens.

Mr. Maltbie maintains that the Queens Borough Gas and Electric Company had not been able to show documentary proof that it owned the Taylor franchise.[1] The chart of the history of the transfer of this franchise puts a question-mark at the first alleged transfer from Taylor to one Seely. As has been indicated, also, the table stated that there were transfers, but put a question-mark by the statement. The title of the company to the Myers franchise as well, was held to be in doubt: "No documentary evidence was produced by the company to show that the Myers grant ever became the property of the Rockaway Electric Light Company."[2] The situation is summed up as follows:

> Granting that the Rockaway Electric Light Company had title to the Myers franchise and that it was properly transferred by Bennett as a receiver to Rossiter by the deed of sale dated July 26, 1897, it appears that Rossiter entered into a contract with the Queens Borough Electric Light and Power Company under date of June 30, 1898, by which he agreed to transfer this franchise. The Queens Borough Gas and Electric Company was unable, however, to furnish the Commission a copy of the actual transfer which it is claimed took place. In lieu of this the company furnished a confirmatory or quit-claim deed, executed by Rossiter on May 28, 1908, more than a year after the Commission had called the company's attention to the apparent defects in its title to this franchise.[3]

[1] Maltbie, *Franchises of Electrical Corporations*, p. 152.

[2] *Ibid.*, p. 153.

[3] *Ibid.*, p. 153.

Concerning the franchise granted by the trustees of the village of Far Rockaway to the Rockaway Electric Light Company, the Report stated that no proof had been presented to show that the original grantee had complied with the franchise terms requiring the separate approval of the village president or the filing of the indemnity bond; and that "no evidence whatever has been presented by the present operating company to show that this franchise ever passed from the possession of the company to which it was granted originally." [1] The record of transfers of the franchise granted to the Citizens Lighting Company is clear, and may be traced in the corporate history of the present operating company. Finally, the two franchises granted to Van Wyck Rossiter were transferred by him to the Queens Borough Electric Light and Power Company. As the corporate history of the Queens Borough Gas and Electric Company shows, the Queens Borough Electric Light and Power Company was later merged into the present operating company.

After consolidation with the city of New York, the village of New Brighton (town of Castleton) became ward one of the borough of Richmond; the town of Middletown became ward two; the town of Northfield became ward three; the town of Southfield became ward four; and the town of Westfield became ward five. The village of Edgewater made up parts of the towns of Middletown and Southfield; the village of Port Richmond, a part of the town of Northfield; and the village of Tottenville, a part of the town of Westfield. The franchises discussed in this chapter are one from the village of New Brighton (the New York and Staten Island Electric Company franchise); one from the village of Edgewater (the New York and Staten Island Electric Company contract); one from the village

[1] Maltbie, *Franchises of Electrical Corporations*, p. 153.

of Port Richmond (the Richmond County Electric Light Company franchise); one from the town of Northfield (the Lisk franchise, a franchise granted by Lisk, the commissioner of highways of the road district of the town, to the Richmond County Electric Light Company); two from the town of Southfield (the highway commissioners' franchise and the town board grant); one from the village of Tottenville; and two from the town of Westfield (the highway commissioners' franchise and the town board franchise).[1] They are tabulated in part as follows:

TABLE IX—ANALYSIS OF ELECTRIC LIGHT FRANCHISES HELD OR CLAIMED BY RICHMOND LIGHT AND RAILROAD COMPANY—OLD VILLAGE GRANTS[2]

Original grantee.	Richmond County Electric Light Co.	New York and Staten Island Electric Company.	New York and Staten Island Electric Company.	New York and Staten Island Electric Company.
Local authority.	Board of village trustees.	Board of village trustees.	Board of village trustees.	Board of village trustees.
Date of franchise.	September 10, 1896.	March 9, 1897.	April 6, 1897.	November 17, 1897.
Territory covered by franchise.	Village of Port Richmond.	Village of New Brighton.	Village of Edgewater.	Village of Tottenville.
Duration of franchise.			Twenty years from date.	Twenty-five years.
Scope of franchise.	Electricity for light, heat and power.	Lighting by electricity and using electricity for heat and power.	Lighting by electricity and using electricity for heat and power.	Lighting by electricity and furnishing electricity for heat and power.

[1] Mr. Maltbie speaks of the uncertainty regarding the proper franchise-granting authorities in the towns of Southfield and Westfield. Both the town board and the highway commissioners granted franchises in these towns. *Franchises of Electrical Corporations*, p. 205.

[2] Maltbie, *Franchises of Electrical Corporations*, pp. 209-211. The table is here presented only in part.

TABLE IX—ANALYSIS OF ELECTRIC LIGHT FRANCHISES HELD OR CLAIMED BY RICHMOND LIGHT AND RAILROAD COMPANY—OLD VILLAGE GRANTS (*Concluded*)

Grant exclusive.	No.			No.
Grantee's "successors or assigns" recognized in franchise.	No.	Yes.	Yes.	Yes.
Number of times franchise has been transferred.	Two.	One.	One.	One.

TABLE X—ANALYSIS OF ELECTRIC LIGHT FRANCHISES HELD OR CLAIMED BY RICHMOND LIGHT AND RAILROAD COMPANY—OLD TOWN GRANTS [1]

Original grantee.	Richmond County Electric Light Co.	New York and Staten Island Electric Co.	New York and Staten Island Electric Co.	New York and Staten Island Electric Co.	New York and Staten Island Electric Co.
Local authority.	Commissioner of highways.	Highway commissioners.	Town Board.	Highway commissioners.	Town Board.
Date of franchise.	January 14, 1897.	May 25 and May 26, 1897; amended Dec. 29, 1897.	August 30, 1897.	June 2 and 16, 1897; amended Sept. 1, 1897.	Sept. 23, 1897.

[1] Maltbie, *Franchises of Electrical Corporations*, pp. 212-214. The table is presented only in part.

TABLE X—ANALYSIS OF ELECTRIC LIGHT FRANCHISES HELD OR CLAIMED BY RICHMOND LIGHT AND RAILROAD COMPANY—OLD TOWN GRANTS (*Continued*)

Territory covered by franchise.	Town of Northfield outside of village of Port Richmond.	Town of Southfield outside of village of Edgewater.	Town of Southfield outside of village of Edgewater.	Town of Westfield outside of village of Tottenville. Streets to be selected by company. Amended Sept. 1, 1897, to include all streets.	Town of Westfield outside of village of Tottenville.
Duration of franchise.	" Shall not be revocable except by due process of law."	Originally unlimited; made " perpetual " by amendment Dec. 29, 1897.			
Scope of franchise.	Electric lighting and power.	Lighting by electricity; using electricity for heat and power and furnishing heat, power and light to public and private parties.	Electricity for light, heat and power " for commercial purposes only."	Lighting by electricity; using electricity for heat and power and furnishing light, heat and power to public or private parties. Not to include right to run trolley cars or supply motive power therefor without further consent.	Lighting by electricity and furnishing electricity for heat and power.

TABLE X—ANALYSIS OF ELECTRIC LIGHT FRANCHISES HELD OR CLAIMED BY RICHMOND LIGHT AND RAILROAD COMPANY—OLD TOWN GRANTS (*Concluded*)

Compensation in money.			One-half of one per cent of gross receipts per annum for first ten years, and one per cent thereafter; payable annually by Jan. 15.		
Grant exclusive.				No.	
Grantee's "successors or assigns" recognized in franchise.	No.	No.	Yes.	No.	No.
Number of times franchise has been transferred.	Two.	One.	One.	One.	One.

The New York and Staten Island Electric Light Company was the original grantee of seven of the nine franchises tabulated. It was the contention of the engineer in charge of the city division of franchises at the time Mr. Maltbie made his report, that the company could establish claim to only one of the seven; namely, the franchise granted on March 9, 1897, by the board of trustees of the village of New Brighton. He maintained that since the certificate of incorporation of the New York and Staten Island Electric Company did not include the right, original or amended, to carry on an electric business in any place but the town of Castleton (coterminous with the village of New Brighton), the company had no capacity to acquire local consent to operate in the villages of Edgewater and Tottenville, or the towns of Southfield and Westfield. The conclusion is apparent. If the theory is correct, the Richmond Light and Railroad Company, the present operating company, does not own the six franchises enumerated; it could not purchase from the New York and Staten Island Electric Company what the latter company did not rightfully own. The engineer's theory extends even to the two remaining franchises, the one granted to the Richmond County Electric Light Company by the board of trustees of the village of Port Richmond, and the one granted by the commissioner of highways of the town of Northfield, since the New York and Staten Island Electric Company would not have the right to receive them from the original grantee.

Another question arises as to the validity of those franchises granted after the date of approval of the charter of Greater New York. The question affects four of the franchises held by the present operating company, but will be discussed in another connection.

There is a further question in regard to the validity of certain franchises on account of the uncertainty as to what constituted the municipal authorities of towns or separate road districts within the meaning of the statute requiring their consent for the operations of electric light companies. If the Town Board was the proper authority, then franchises granted by the Highway Commissioners would be ineffectual. If, on the other hand, the Highway Commissioners were the proper authority, franchises granted by the Town Board would be invalid. If the consent of both Town Board and Highway Commissioners was required, then franchises granted by the two authorities on different terms and conditions would fall into an uncertain category. These questions apply primarily to the town of Northfield, where only the highway commissioner gave his consent, and to the towns of Southfield and Westfield, where both bodies gave franchises but on different conditions.[1]

The charter of Greater New York was approved on May 4, 1897. Greater New York came into existence on January 1, 1898. Five of the franchises now held by the Richmond Light and Railroad Company, two held by the Queens Borough Gas and Electric Company, and two claimed by the New York and Queens Electric Light and Power Company were granted by local authorities after May 4, 1897. Three of the five franchises granted after May 4, 1897, and now held by the Richmond Light and Railroad Company, have no time-limit expressed; a fourth was made perpetual, "unless the courts shall finally decree that under the provisions of the charter of Greater New York . . . this board had not the power . . . to grant the same to the said company in perpetuity;" and the fifth was limited to twenty-five years. Neither of the two franchises granted after that date and now held by the Queens Borough Gas and Electric Company has any time-limit expressed. One of the franchises granted after May 4, 1897, and now held by the New York and Queens Electric Light and Power Company, was granted for an initial period of twenty-five years, with the right to renewal, after revaluation, for another twenty-five years.[2] The other, granted by the town board of Jamaica, on November 26, 1897, to the Jamaica Electric Light Company is for a term of forty-five years.

[1] Maltbie, *Franchises of Electrical Corporations*, p. 205.

[2] By error the table gives an initial period of twenty-six years.

Mr. Maltbie cites the case of Blaschko *v.* Wurster,[1] in which the court held that "after May 4, 1897, . . . no franchise could be granted by any local authority within the present limits of the Greater City except in accordance with the provisions of this charter."[2] Section 73 of the charter approved on May 4, 1897, limited the initial franchise period to twenty-five years, with a renewal period aggregating another twenty-five years. Referring to the franchises granted after May 4, 1897, for more than the initial period permitted under the provisions of the charter of Greater New York, and the franchises granted after that date with no time-limit expressed, the Report states:

> It may be claimed that these franchises are valid but that the statutory provision limiting franchise terms to twenty-five years applies to them. Under the decision of the court above referred to, they certainly are not perpetual.[3]

The franchise with the forty-five year term was considered by Mr. Maltbie to be invalid in whole or in part, since it was not in conformity with the charter provision which allows an initial period of but twenty-five years.

Brief mention must be made of the questions of franchises by acquiescence, franchises by private contract, and franchises by annexation. If the local authorities permit a company to extend its services into an area and maintain its pipes or wires there, it is frequently held that the company obtains thereby a franchise by acquiescence. It would seem that the theory of acquiescence might be advanced with respect to a company whose franchise rights had expired with regard to the area in question, but which had continued operating without any protest from the local authorities; or

[1] Blaschko *v.* Wurster, 156 N. Y. 437.

[2] Maltbie, *Franchises of Electrical Corporations,* p. 18.

[3] *Ibid.,* p. 19. *These franchises* are the ones without time limit.

with respect to a company whose franchise rights in the disputed area were either originally entirely absent or were at a later date seriously questioned as to validity. Those upholding the theory of acquiescence maintain that the company obtains consent when the local authorities either openly favor or tacitly approve occupation of the area for which no formal grant has been obtained by the company, even though that consent has not been offered in writing, or by any formal resolution. The theory of franchise by private contract is briefly explained:

According to this theory, if a company were to produce and distribute current upon its own land, or were to make a contract with a real-estate company for such purposes, using only private property and never any street or highway which had been dedicated to the public, and if later public streets were laid out where the company had its mains and wires, such company would *ipso facto* come to have a franchise under the terms of the private contract as originally made, even though the local authority within whose area these streets were located had not granted a franchise or any right whatsoever.[1]

There is a provision in the charter of Greater New York against the territorial expansion of existing franchise rights; consequently, the question of franchises by annexation does not arise with respect to the enlargement of the boundaries of the city of New York on January 1, 1898. But the theory is of interest in regard to the district annexed to the old city of New York June 6, 1895. Concerning the application of the theory, the report said: [2]

For example, all of the valid franchises of the New York Edison Company were granted prior to the time when that portion of The Bronx east of the Bronx river was made a part

[1] Maltbie, *Franchises of Electrical Corporations*, p. 14.

[2] *Ibid.*, pp. 14, 15.

of the City of New York. The company claims that the annexation of this area *ipso facto* gave the company the right to supply in that territory. No legislation nor court decisions were cited in support of this claim, and the company is not operating in the annexed district, which is supplied by the Bronx Gas and Electric Company and the Westchester Lighting Company. If this theory is good law, the United Electric Light and Power Company and its subsidiaries, and possibly the Long Acre Electric Light and Power Company have rights to operate in The Bronx east of the Bronx river. An affirmative answer to the question would also extend the franchises granted by the former city of Brooklyn to the Edison Electric Illuminating Company of Brooklyn, the Kings County Electric Light and Power Company, and the State Electric Light and Power Company to cover not only the territory which was included in the city of Brooklyn at the time these grants were made, but also all the outlying districts that were later annexed to the city. It is even claimed by the Edison Company of Brooklyn that the old Pope, Sewall & Company franchise of 1884, afterwards used by the Citizens Electric Illuminating Company, was extended automatically by the annexation of territory to the city to include all that portion of the present Borough of Brooklyn except Wards 13 to 19 as they existed at the time of the grant.

CHAPTER III

DOUBTFUL AND INVALID FRANCHISES

IN addition to the electrical franchises discussed in the preceding chapter, attention must be directed to certain franchises that are unclaimed, are claimed without sufficient evidence, are uncertain in status, are not strictly electric-lighting grants, have been lost, have been superseded, have expired, or are clearly invalid.

Sixteen franchises that fall within one or more of these categories were granted by the old city of New York while its area was limited to Manhattan Island and that part of The Bronx west of the Bronx river. These include the Electric Lines franchise, the first Harlem franchise, the grant made to the Waterhouse Electric and Manufacturing Company, the Mutual franchise, and the twelve franchises granted between 1887 and 1897 by the board of electrical control.[1] The Electric Lines franchise, not strictly an electric-lighting grant, was obtained in 1883 by the New York Electric Lines Company. It was the purpose of the company to lay wires underground and lease them to telephone, telegraph, and electric light companies.[2] The first Harlem

[1] Maltbie, *Franchises of Electrical Corporations in Greater New York*, pp. 30-44.

[2] *Ibid.*, pp. 32, 218. The commissioners of electrical subways, appointed after the passing of an act in 1884 requiring telegraph and electric light companies in the city of New York to put their wires underground, contracted with the Consolidated Telegraph and Electrical Subway Company for construction of electrical subways. The right of the New York Electrical Lines Company to construct subways was held by the courts to have lapsed in 1886. (New York Electric Lines Company *v.* Ellison, 188 N. Y. 523).

franchise, granted December 7, 1886, gave the Harlem Lighting Company authority to operate in a limited territory in Manhattan Island and in that part of The Bronx west of the Bronx river. Although held by the New York Edison Company, it is to all intents and purposes superseded by the Harlem Lighting grant of May 31, 1887.[1] The grant made to the Waterhouse Electric and Manufacturing Company was one of the six franchises granted by a single resolution of the board of aldermen May 31, 1887, and known as the omnibus electric franchise. This grant to the Waterhouse Company appears to be lost. "In fact, a thorough search of the indexes in the Secretary of State's office has failed to show any reference to the incorporation of a company in this state [New York] under that name." [2] The franchise granted to the Mutual Electric Illuminating Company on June 7, 1887, seems also to be lost.

It was held by the court of appeals in a decision rendered on January 7, 1907,[3] that the board of electrical control had been unwarranted in assuming the franchise-granting authority of the old city of New York after June 7, 1887. Consequently, the grants between 1887 and 1897 became clearly illegal. Four of the clearly invalid grants were made to predecessors of the New York Edison Company: the grant of October 19, 1888, to the Manhattan Electric Light Company, Limited; [4] the grant of February 8, 1893,

[1] *Supra*, p. 58.

[2] Maltbie, *Franchises of Electrical Corporations*, p. 44.

[3] West Side Electric Company *v.* The Consolidated Telegraph and Electrical Subway Company, 187 N. Y. 58 (1907). This decision is discussed in Mr. Maltbie's report, p. 42.

[4] This grant is not enumerated in the list of "franchises" (p. 42) reported in *Franchises of Electrical Corporations* as granted by the board of electrical control. It is mentioned, however, in a later connection (p. 48) as being granted to a predecessor of the New York Edison Company. In reality, therefore, there were thirteen "fran-

to the New York Heat, Light and Power Company; the grant of November 12, 1894, to the Block Lighting and Power Company No. 1; and the grant of June 7, 1895, to the Madison Square Light Company. One of the grants was made on September 20, 1887, "to the Safety Electric Light and Power Company, the original name under which the United Electric Light and Power Company was incorporated."[1] Another grant was made to a predecessor of the Westchester Lighting Company, the grant of December 31, 1897, to the Pelham Electric Light and Power Company. The remaining invalid franchises may be disposed of briefly. One was granted on October 29, 1896, to the Fleischauer Electric Light and Power Company; one on November 12, 1896, to the West Side Electric Company; one on December 7, 1897, to the Metropolitan Electric Light, Heat and Power Company; and three on December 31, 1897, to the Greater New York Electric Light and Power Company, the Commercial Light, Heat and Power Company, and the Colonial Electric Company of New York, respectively.

Among the franchises granted for the territory now occupied by the New York and Queens Electric Light and Power Company were two that have been superseded by a grant held by the present operating company, four that have apparently never been transferred to this company, and two contracts for public lighting that have expired. These grants were made by the village of Flushing and by the town and the village of Jamaica.

Certain streets of the village of Flushing were covered

chises" granted by the board of electrical control. The minutes of the board for the date, October 19, 1888, state the grant of two franchises, namely, one to the Manhattan Electric Light Company, Limited, and one to the Electric Power Company.

[1] Maltbie, *Franchises of Electrical Corporations*, p. 58.

by a grant made on November 19, 1889, to a corporation to be organized by Joseph Dykes and his associates. The conditions imposed dealt with the questions of poles, time of beginning operation, indemnity bond, acceptance of grant, and compliance with regulations of the board of trustees. The purpose of granting the franchise was avowed to be the desire to give the inhabitants the opportunity to test the value of an electric light and power system. The grant was revocable by the board of trustees at their discretion. For all practical purposes this Dykes grant was superseded [1] by the grant of 1892, taken up in the next paragraph.

The grant of April 5, 1892, made by the board of trustees of the village of Flushing to the Flushing Electric Light and Power Company, was a general franchise for furnishing electric light and power. The franchise period was set at twenty-five years. This grant, in turn, was superseded by the franchise of January 18, 1897, granted to the same company.[2]

On December 12, 1895, the commissioners of highways of the town of Jamaica [3] granted to the Woodhaven Electric Light Company a franchise for distributing electricity

[1] "If any rights remain under the original Dykes grant they are now held by the New York and Queens Electric Light and Power Company." Maltbie, *Franchises of Electrical Corporations*, p. 107.

[2] *Supra*, p. 69.

[3] Another grant made by the town of Jamaica, this time by its town board, is shown by the minutes of the board for December 23, 1892. The Report calls attention to this grant to erect poles, made to the West Jamaica Electric Light Company, and adds:

"A reference to the company's application is found in the minutes of December 31, 1891, but no light is cast upon the specific proposal made by the company. It should be noted that this franchise was granted at a time prior to the incorporation of the village of Richmond Hill, and would therefore cover the territory later included in the village as well as that portion of the old town of Jamaica covered by later town franchises." Maltbie, *Franchises of Electrical Corporations*, p. 111.

for light, heat and power. This grant has never been used.[1]

No extended analysis is herewith given of the five grants listed under the village of Jamaica.[2] A franchise for electric lighting was granted by the board of trustees on January 7, 1886, to the American Electric Manufacturing Company. The territory covered by its terms included the entire village of Jamaica. "No evidence has been found that the company ever operated under the Jamaica franchise or transferred it to any other person or company."[3] On October 12, 1887, the board of trustees granted a franchise for electric lighting to the Jamaica Gas Light Company. Concerning this grant the Report states:[4]

The New York and Queens Electric Light and Power Company makes no claim to the electric-lighting franchise granted to the Jamaica Gas Light Company on October 12, 1887. There is no record among the papers filed with the Public Service Commission or in the minutes of the Jamaica village trustees, so far as we have been able to find, showing that the Jamaica Gas Light Company's electric franchise was ever transferred.

The board of trustees granted on October 12, 1887, to Jesse Browne, Jr., and associates, a franchise for electric lighting. "No record of the corporate identity of Jesse Browne, Jr., and his associates, and no trace of any construction or operation under the Browne franchise, or of

[1] Maltbie, *Franchises of Electrical Corporations*, p. 112.

[2] Mention is made of an electric lighting contract between the village and the National Electric Manufacturing and Construction Company, October 1, 1890, and of a transfer of this contract to the Jamaica Gas Light Company in 1891. The latter company did not operate its electric light plant after 1893. Maltbie, *Franchises of Electrical Corporations*, p. 118.

[3] *Ibid.*, p. 117.

[4] *Ibid.*, p. 119.

the transfer of this franchise to any other person or company has been found." [1]

Two contracts for public lighting were executed between the board of trustees of the village of Jamaica and the Jamaica Electric Light Company, one for a period of three years,[2] and the other for a period of five years. The first contract was executed on September 25, 1893; the second, September 16, 1896. On December 29, 1897, the company petitioned for an electric light franchise for a period of forty-five years. The petition was not granted.

The board of trustees of the village of Rockaway Beach granted, on August 25, 1897, a franchise for electric lighting on five streets to the Seaside Amusement Company. On December 31, 1897, the board passed two resolutions, one granting to William G. Wainwright or his assigns the consent to carry on the business of furnishing electric light and power for stationary motors in private and public buildings west of Holland Avenue, and the other granting a like request to Louis Hammel in the streets and avenues and public parks east of Holland Avenue.[3] Both grants were, of course, confined to the limits of Rockaway Beach. They are listed as the Wainwright-Hammell franchises. The Report states:

It is believed that the franchise granted to William G. Wainwright is now held by the Seaside Electric Light, Heat and Power Company, which was incorporated July 9, 1900, with

[1] Maltbie, *Franchises of Electrical Corporations*, p. 119.

[2] The first contract was executed between the village and one John Williamson, who became president of the Jamaica Electric Light Company, incorporated October 13, 1893. Maltbie, *Franchises of Electrical Corporations*, p. 121.

[3] The former village of Rockaway Beach is a part of the fifth ward of the borough of Queens in which the Queens Borough Gas and Electric Company is operating.

three Wainwrights as members of its first board of directors. This company operated to a limited extent some years ago, but is now dormant. . . .

The villages of New Brighton, Edgewater, and Port Richmond and the towns of Northfield and Middleton granted franchises to be considered in this chapter in connection with the present borough of Richmond. Under the franchises of the village of New Brighton come the Richmond Light, Heat and Power Company, Limited, contract and franchise of 1888; and the Electric Power Company contracts and franchise, 1893 to 1897. Listed under the franchises of the village of Edgewater are the Richmond Light, Heat and Power Company, Limited, contracts from 1887 to 1893; the Electric Power Company's contracts, 1893 to 1896; and the Richmond Borough Electric Company contract of 1897. Under the franchises of the village of Port Richmond are the Richmond Light, Heat and Power Company, Limited, franchise and permits, 1887 to 1892; the Staten Island Light, Heat and Power Company contract, 1889 to 1893; the Charles H. Ingalls and Port Richmond Electric Company franchise and contract, 1894; the New York and Staten Island Electric Company contract, 1897; and the Electrical Subway franchise, 1897. The town of Northfield grants are the town board franchise of 1897 to the New York and Staten Island Electric Company, and the Melvin Subway franchise of 1897. Last of all comes the lighting contract of the town of Middletown in 1897.

The only one of the many provisions of the contract for electric lighting executed between the village of New Brighton and the Richmond Light, Heat and Power Company, Limited, on March 12, 1888, which need be repeated here is the clause which provided that the contract should not be transferred or assigned. The company became bankrupt. "Apparently the company's franchises perished with it and are not at the present time claimed by anybody." [1] The contracts of the village with the Electric Power Company of Staten Island extended over about four years. This company also went into bankruptcy. Through its receiver, the company entered into a contract, on August 7, 1894, for lighting the village. One of the many conditions of this contract was that it could not be assigned or transferred. Another contract was entered into between the village and the receiver on May 22, 1895. Commenting upon transfers of property and franchises made by the receiver for the company, the Report states: [2]

> Apparently there was no franchise received by this company or its receiver from the village of New Brighton that could have been transferred. Indeed it would appear that the franchise contained in the contract of August 7, 1894, expired July 1, 1897, and if it did not actually expire at that time became revocable at the option of the village authorities.

The contract of the village of Edgewater in 1887 with the Richmond Light, Heat and Power Company, Limited, was for public lighting. Other contracts for public lighting were entered into between the village and the company between 1887 and 1893. The company, as has been indicated, went into bankruptcy.[3] In January, 1897, the board of trustees

[1] Maltbie, *Franchises of Electrical Corporations*, p. 164.

[2] *Ibid.*, p. 165.

[3] Concerning the Electric Power Company of Staten Island's contracts from 1893 to 1896 the Report states (p. 169):

"The Electric Power Company of Staten Island, which appears to have succeeded in November, 1892, to some of the property of the Richmond Light, Heat and Power Company, Limited, went into bankruptcy in May, 1893. Its receiver, Albert B. Boardman, was awarded a contract by the Board of Trustees of the village of Edgewater on July 11, 1893, and others in later years . . . No copy of any of these contracts has been found."

of the village contracted with the Richmond Borough Electric Company to furnish electric light for the remainder of the fiscal year ending on May 31, 1897.

The franchise and permits granted by the village authorities of the village of Port Richmond between 1887 and 1892 to the Richmond Light, Heat and Power Company, Limited, will not be discussed in detail. The Report states:[1]

The franchises of the Richmond Light, Heat and Power Company, Limited, do not seem to be claimed by the present operating company, as none of these papers were filed with the Public Service Commission with the company's franchise documents, and no reference was made to the Richmond Light, Heat and Power Company either in the present company's correspondence in regard to documents or at the hearings.

In the last part of 1889, the village authorities of the village of Port Richmond agreed to permit the Staten Island Light, Heat and Power Company to execute a contract which had originally been granted to the Montauk Construction Company. It is believed that the Staten Island Light, Heat and Power Company furnished public lighting in the village until 1894. Concerning the relation of these contracts to the Richmond Light and Railroad Company, the Report states:[2]

The present operating company did not file with the Public Service Commission with its franchise papers any of the documents of the Staten Island Light, Heat and Power Company, and does not appear to claim any franchise rights originally acquired by the latter company.

On April 26, 1894, a contract for lighting the streets of

[1] Maltbie, *Franchises of Electrical Corporations*, p. 174.

[2] *Ibid.*, p. 175.

the village of Port Richmond was entered into between the village board and Charles H. Ingalls. The contract stipulated that the agreement should terminate five years from the date of its execution. On July 6, 1894, the board agreed to permit Ingalls to assign the contract to the Port Richmond Electric Company. The Report concludes: [1]

> Any transferable rights of the Port Richmond Electric Company were acquired in 1897 by the New York and Staten Island Electric Company, but the present operating company has not filed with the Public Service Commission among its franchise documents a copy of the Ingalls contract, and does not appear to claim franchise rights under it.

The contract of September 7, 1897, between the board of village trustees of Port Richmond and the New York and Staten Island Electric Company was executed about two years before the close of the period set forth in the Ingalls contract. The Report says: [2]

> This contract did not of itself grant any continuing franchise rights. It recognized, however, the validity of the general franchise granted to the Richmond County Electric Light Company and of its transfer to the New York and Staten Island Electric Company.

On February 16, 1897, the board of trustees of the village of Port Richmond authorized Joseph Pearce, Howard Bull, and five others to construct and operate subways in the village for "wires, pipes, conductors, conduits, fixtures, appliances and appurtenances for conducting and distributing electricity, gas, water, oil, fluids, wires and steam." The grantees incorporated as the Richmond Borough Subway Company under the laws of the state of New Jersey. Commenting upon the franchise, the Report states: [3]

[1] Maltbie, *Franchises of Electrical Corporations*, p. 176.

[2] *Ibid.*, p. 179.

[3] *Ibid.*, p. 180.

No record has been found of any activity under this franchise or a similar one granted by the local authorities of the town of Northfield, to which reference will be made later in this report. The present status of the Richmond Borough Subway Company and of the rights obtained under this franchise has not been ascertained.

On April 12, 1897, the town board of the town of Northfield resolved that they execute a contract for public lighting with the New York and Staten Island Electric Company. The resolution was accepted by the company on April 20, 1897. There is on file with the city bureau of franchises another contract copy, uncertified, purporting to have been executed on April 20, 1897, between the town board and the same company, allowing for public and private lighting, and stipulating that the agreement terminate April 1, 1907. On April 23, 1897, the town board passed another resolution regarding conditions required to make the grants operative, such as the filing of a bond. The Report sums up the account of the three contracts: [1]

The present operating company does not, however, appear to make any claims of any franchise or contract derived from the action of the town board on April 12, April 20 or April 23, 1897. At least, no documents referring to such action or claiming franchise rights thereunder have been filed with the Public Service Commission among the documents by the Richmond Light and Railroad Company.

The remaining franchise to be listed under those granted by the town of Northfield is the Melvin Subway franchise of 1897, similar to the electrical subway franchise granted by the village of Port Richmond. Concerning the Melvin Subway franchise, the Report states: [2]

[1] Maltbie, *Franchises of Electrical Corporations*, p. 184.

[2] *Ibid.*, p. 184.

We have found no record to show that a corporation was ever formed to exercise this franchise, that the franchise was, as a matter of fact, exercised, or that it is now claimed by any one as a valid franchise.

The only other item to be considered concerns the old town of Middletown. The Report states: [1]

The Richmond Light and Railroad Company is operating there, but was unable to furnish the Commission any conclusive evidence that it, or any of its predecessors, ever received a franchise from the town authorities. In the absence of a franchise the company filed certain extracts from the minutes of the town board.

These extracts indicate that a resolution of December 31, 1897, authorized a contract with the New York Staten Island Electric Company. The Report continues: [2]

No record has been found of any electric-lighting franchise granted by the town of Middletown, and no copy of the contract authorized December 31, 1897, with the New York and Staten Island Electric Company, if such a contract was in fact executed, has as yet been discovered.

[1] Maltbie, *Franchises of Electrical Corporations*, p. 184.

[2] *Ibid.*, p. 185.

CHAPTER IV

THE GENERAL MANUFACTURING CORPORATIONS ACT

THE validity of the franchises under which electric lighting is carried on in the borough of Brooklyn is challenged.[1] The Edison Electric Illuminating Company of Brooklyn was merged in January, 1919, into the Kings County Electric Light and Power Company, but it is essential to discuss the basis of the challenge in its relation to the companies as they existed before the merger.

The Edison Electric Illuminating Company of Brooklyn based its system upon five directly or indirectly controlled franchises. A franchise for electric lighting was granted to Charles Cooper and Company by a resolution of the common council of the city of Brooklyn on May 12, 1884. The territory specified in that original grant covered the parts of the city at present embraced in wards 13 to 19 inclusive and in wards 27 and 28 in the borough of Brooklyn.[2] The franchise was transferred to the Municipal Electric Light Company, a company incorporated on August 2, 1884, under the general manufacturing corporations law of 1848, and merged on October 30, 1899, into the Edison Electric Illuminating Company of Brooklyn.[3]

[1] Clements *v.* Edison Company, reported in the *New York Law Journal*, July 26, 1917; Smith *v.* Edison Company, vacating of injunction reported in *New York Law Journal*, August 30, 1917; objections of city to merger of Edison Company into Kings Company, stated in *Answer of City of New York* in case no. 2351.

[2] Wards 27 and 28 were created out of ward 18 in 1892.

[3] The company will be referred to as the Edison Company.

By the same resolution of May 12, 1884, the common council of the city of Brooklyn granted to Pope, Sewall and Company a franchise for electric lighting. The territory covered by the precise terms of the original grant included what is now embraced in wards 1 to 12, and wards 20 to 25 inclusive. The franchise was later acquired by the Citizens Electric Illuminating Company of Brooklyn, a company incorporated on December 13, 1883, under the general manufacturing corporations law of 1848, and merged on October 30, 1899, into the Edison Company.

On October 29, 1888, the common council of the city of Brooklyn passed a resolution granting a franchise for electric lighting and power to the Edison Company. The territory specified in the grant was the city of Brooklyn. At that time the city of Brooklyn included the first twenty-eight wards of the present borough of Brooklyn. The Edison Company was incorporated on March 9, 1887, under the general manufacturing corporations law of 1848.

A franchise for light, heat and power was granted on June 11, 1894, by resolution of the common council of the city of Brooklyn to the Kings County Electric Light and Power Company. The city of Brooklyn was the territory specified by the terms of the franchise. At the time the franchise became effective, June 23, 1894, the city embraced the present wards 1 to 29 inclusive and ward 31. The Kings County Electric Light and Power Company [1] was incorporated on June 26, 1890, under the general manufacturing corporations law of 1848. On October 30, 1899, the company leased its franchise to the Edison Company.

A franchise for lighting, heat and power was granted to the State Electric Light and Power Company by resolution of the common council of the city of Brooklyn on December

[1] The Kings County Electric Light and Power Company will be referred to as the Kings County Company.

30, 1895. The territory stipulated in the franchise was the city of Brooklyn. On January 1, 1896, the city of Brooklyn annexed the outlying town of Flatlands, an area comprising ward 32 of the present borough of Brooklyn.[1] The State Electric Light and Power Company was incorporated on December 7, 1891, under article six of the transportation corporations law. Its franchise was transferred by sale to P. C. Anderson. Anderson transferred his bid to the Amsterdam Electric Light, Heat and Power Company, a company incorporated on April 12, 1897, under article six of the transportation corporations law. As to the extent of control which the Edison Company exerted[2] over the franchise transferred to the Amsterdam Electric Light, Heat and Power Company, the final word cannot be spoken; litigation is now pending (March, 1919) involving precisely that question.

In the detailed discussion of the challenged franchises, the term "special franchise" is used as a synonym of the expression "municipal franchise." The use is justified in part by reason of the fact that the city of New York has no means of knowing precisely which franchises are being used by the company as authority for operation. However, all the franchises controlled directly or indirectly have been assailed as to their validity.

From the foregoing survey of special franchises in the system of the Edison Company, it will be observed that two of the companies concerned were incorporated under article six of the transportation corporations law. Attention will first be directed to the franchises connected with these two

1 The chief territorial question involved is whether the franchises that were granted for the city of Brooklyn were automatically extended to cover territory that was subsequently annexed to the city.

2 The Edison Company is spoken of in the past tense because it was merged in 1919 into the Kings County Company.

companies, the State Electric Light and Power Company and the Amsterdam Electric Light, Heat and Power Company.[1]

In the early part of 1911 the board of estimate and apportionment attempted to pass a resolution revoking the franchise granted on December 30, 1895, by the common council of the city of Brooklyn to the State Company. An action in equity was begun by the Amsterdam Company and the Edison Company to enjoin the board from adopting the resolution. Mr. Delancey Nicoll was appointed by the court as referee. In the proceedings carried on before the referee, the defendants relied for evidence upon the results of an investigation made by the bureau of franchises of the board of estimate and apportionment. It was contended that the investigation had brought out the following facts:[2]

(1) That the State Company had wholly failed to comply with the provisions of the franchise in that it had never supplied a public or private consumer with electricity for light, heat or power; that it had never constructed a foot of conduit nor applied to the administrative officials of the city for a permit for such purpose; that it had never filed a bond necessary to be filed before construction, nor filed a map, nor paid the city the sum required to be paid under the franchise.

(2) That the Amsterdam Company had never obtained the consent of the local authorities of Brooklyn for the laying of electrical conductors; and that no valid assignment had ever

[1] These two companies will be referred to as the State Company and the Amsterdam Company.

[2] *Answer of the City of New York in the Matter of the Petition of the Kings County Electric Light and Power Company for the Permission and Approval of the Public Service Commission of the State of New York for the First District to Merge the Edison Electric Illuminating Company of Brooklyn into and with Itself and to Execute a general Mortgage to be Designated as Its "General Mortgage" upon all Its Plant and Property.* (Case no. 2351), pp. 13-14.

been made by the State Company to the Amsterdam Company of the franchise granted [to the State Company]; that even assuming that a valid assignment had been made, the Amsterdam Company had never complied with the provisions of the franchise by constructing one mile of conduit per year; and that in 1899 the company had wholly abandoned the plant and property and discontinued operation.

(3) That the Edison Company had never merged or consolidated with the Amsterdam Company, and even if the latter company had a valid franchise, that such franchise was never acquired by the Edison Company and that the only interest of the latter in the Amsterdam Company was a part ownership of the capital stock.

Proceedings were carried on for a number of years. The referee filed a report in January, 1916. The plaintiffs moved for an order to remit the report for amendment and correction. The motion to remit to the referee was granted by Mr. Justice Greenbaum in December, 1916.[1] The amended report of the referee was dated March 19, 1917. In April, 1917,[2]

Judgment was entered . . . restraining the Mayor of the City of New York, the members of the Board of Estimate and Apportionment and the City of New York "from taking any legal or other action to prevent the plaintiff Amsterdam Electric Light, Heat and Power Company from exercising the rights and privileges granted in said municipal consent or franchise, in the manner therein provided, for any cause or causes alleged to have existed, or heretofore existing, prior to the date of this judgment." And the complaint of the Edison Company was dismissed upon the ground that its relationship to the Amsterdam Company was merely that of a stockholder and

[1] *New York Law Journal*, December 15, 1916.

[2] Comment on judgment as made by Mr. Justice Benedict in opinion in the *New York Law Journal*, July 26, 1917, in the case of Clements *v.* Edison Company.

that it failed to prove that it leased the franchise of the Amsterdam Company or operated under it in any way.

The decision satisfied neither plaintiffs nor defendants. Both sides appealed. An illuminating view of what the city considers that it has lost and gained by the decision was set forth in its answer:[1]

The referee found that a valid assignment of the rights granted to the State Company had been made to the Amsterdam Company, and that the latter company had substantially complied with the franchise.

Referring to the obligation to construct one mile of conduit each year, the referee said:

"The failure to construct the lines symmetrically one mile each year was at the most an irregularity which the city authorities might waive, and which I think they had waived by the acceptance of the $500, and the other acts and omissions hereinafter referred to. For these reasons I conclude that the franchise was not lost through the manner in which the Amsterdam Company attempted to comply with the provisions of the seventh clause of the resolution.

"It is not necessary for me to consider the exact extent of the right of the Amsterdam Company at the present time. It has at least the right to operate the system which it created prior to July 1, 1900, and that right is entitled to protection in the courts."

In a memorandum submitted with this report the referee said:

"I think the plaintiffs are entitled to have embodied in the main decision the injunctive relief specified in the second conclusion of law proposed by them, and which with the exception that the relief was confined to the Amsterdam Company was found at their request. As I said in my opinion, I did not pass upon the right of either of the plaintiffs with reference to extensions of the system of conduits in existence on July 1, 1900."

[1] *Answer of the City of New York*, pp. 18-19.

At the time the Amsterdam Company abandoned its operations in 1899, it had constructed but 14,200 linear feet of conduit in the streets of Brooklyn.

The City of New York has appealed from the judgment entered on the referee's report, which appeal is now pending; but even assuming that the judgment is affirmed, the only contention of the City that is denied by it is that the franchise of the State Company had been entirely forfeited. By limiting the decision to the point that the company had not lost its right for those conduits constructed prior to 1900, the referee left open and undetermined the question as to whether any right existed to extend the system. It is, however, definitely and unmistakably decided in this case that the Edison Company never acquired by lease, assignment or otherwise, the franchises of the Amsterdam Company, and has therefore no right to exercise them.

The plaintiffs, however, take a different stand toward that "definite and unmistakable" decision. They contend: [1]

The Amsterdam Company is not engaged in business, but the Edison Company which owns all its stock, uses its property and franchises. The Amsterdam Company never constructed any poles or wires in the 30th Ward, its construction being limited to the 13th Ward. Its franchise, however, extends to the whole borough, and is a sufficient authority for the maintenance of structures throughout the borough. The Referee in the above action, however, found that the Edison Company had acquired no title to or interest in the franchises or other property of the Amsterdam Company except to acquire its stocks and bonds. This finding of fact is, we believe, contrary to the evidence in the case, and will be reviewed in the appeal taken by both parties from the judgment entered.

[1] Copy of brief filed by the Edison Company in appeal to the appellate division of the second department from the decision of Mr. Justice Benedict, in the case of Clements *v.* Edison Company (as reported in the *New York Law Journal*, July 26, 1917, p. 11).

The decision of the higher courts has not yet been rendered (March, 1919).

Every remaining franchise of the Edison Company (merged in January, 1919, into the Kings County Company) is being called into question on account of its connection with the general manufacturing corporations act of 1848. The Brooklyn companies incorporated under that law are alleged to be manufacturing corporations, in possession of no valid franchise rights to use the streets. In order to understand the questions involved in this litigation it is necessary briefly to review the statutes that are involved.

On February 16, 1848, there was enacted "An act to authorize the formation of gas light companies." [1] While no need would be served by repeating the act in its entirety, one of the provisions of section 18 may profitably be noted:

> Any corporation formed under this act shall have full power to manufacture and sell and to furnish such quantities of gas as may be required in the city, town or village where the same shall be located for lighting the streets and public and private buildings, or for other purposes; and such corporation shall have full power to lay conductors for conducting gas through the streets, lanes, alleys, and squares in such city, village or town, with the consent of the municipal authorities of said city, village or town and under such reasonable regulations as they may prescribe.

On February 17, 1848, there was passed "An act to authorize the formation of corporations for manufacturing, mining, mechanical and chemical purposes." [2] This act is variously referred to as the general manufacturing corporations act, the manufacturing corporations act, the manufacturing act, and chapter 40 of the laws of 1848. Thirty-one

[1] Laws of 1848, ch. 37.

[2] Laws of 1848, ch. 40.

years later an act was passed [1] which has an important bearing upon recent litigation. It was entitled "An act to authorize gas light companies to use electricity instead of gas for the lighting of streets, public places and public and private buildings in cities, villages and towns within the state." Its four sections were as follows:

Section 1. Any corporation duly organized under the act entitled "An act to authorize the formation of gas light companies," passed February sixteenth, eighteen hundred and forty-eight, and the several acts amendatory thereof, may use electricity instead of gas as the means for lighting streets, avenues, public parks and places, and public and private dwellings of cities, villages and towns within the state.

Section 2. Any such company described in the first section hereof shall have full power to carry on the business of lighting by electricity cities, towns and villages within the state, and the streets, avenues, public parks and places thereof, and public and private dwellings therein; and for the purposes of such businesses to generate and supply electricity, and to make, sell, or lease all machines, instruments, apparatus, and other equipment necessary therefor; and shall also have power to lay, erect and construct suitable wires or other conductors, with the necessary poles, pipes, or other fixtures, in, on, over and under the streets, avenues, public parks and places of such cities, towns or villages, for conducting and distributing electricity with the consent of the municipal authorities thereof, and under such reasonable regulations as they may prescribe.

Section 3. The city of Brooklyn and the county of Kings are hereby exempted from the provisions of this act.

In 1882,[2] this law of 1879 was amended as follows:

Section 1. Section one of chapter five hundred and twelve of the laws of eighteen hundred and seventy-nine, entitled "An

[1] Laws of 1879, ch. 512.

[2] Laws of 1882, ch. 73.

act to authorize gas light companies to use electricity instead of gas for the lighting of streets, public places, and public and private buildings in cities, villages and towns within this state," is hereby amended so as to read as follows:

Section 1. Any corporation duly organized under the act entitled "An act to authorize the formation of gas light companies," passed February sixteenth, eighteen hundred and forty-eight, and the several acts amendatory thereof, and any corporation duly organized under the laws of this state, for manufacturing and using electricity for producing light, heat or power may use electricity as the means of lighting streets, avenues, public parks and places, and public and private dwellings of cities, villages and towns within this state.

Section 2. This act shall take effect immediately.

In the light of this survey of the general incorporation laws, attention may now be directed to the points at issue in the case of Clements *v.* Williams and Pounds.[1] Albert Clements, a resident of the 30th ward of the borough of Brooklyn, applied for a peremptory writ of mandamus to compel Mr. Williams, the commissioner of water supply, gas and electricity, and Mr. Pounds, the president of the borough of Brooklyn, to remove certain electric-light poles and wires in the ward. It was his contention that the Edison Company, the company owning and maintaining those poles and wires, had no franchise rights from either state or city under which to occupy the streets and carry on its business. In January, 1917, action was begun in the supreme court, Kings County. The next month, by an order of the court, following an application made by the commissioner of water supply and the borough president, the Edison and Amsterdam companies were brought into the proceedings as parties defendant. Mr. Justice Benedict, before whom the cause was heard, denied the application for a peremptory

[1] Clements *v.* Edison Company, *New York Law Journal*, July 26, 1917.

writ but ordered that an alternative writ be issued, directing that the poles other than those used for the lighting of the public streets be removed or that cause be shown why the writ ought not to be obeyed.

An appeal was taken from that order by the Edison and Amsterdam companies to the appellate division, second department. Clements obtained a postponement. Later he asked to have the appeal dismissed on the grounds that he was not able to bear the expense. This request was refused. The case is still pending (March, 1919) awaiting argument.

Mr. Justice Benedict's writ was evidently issued because of disagreement as to facts.[1] In his opinion, however, he expresses his views on two of the points of law involved; namely, that the Edison Company received no support from the amendment of 1882, and that the city of Brooklyn had no power under its charter to grant the right to distribute electricity for commercial lighting. But he did not say expressly that incorporation under the general manufacturing corporations act did not give the Edison Company capacity to receive a franchise from municipal authorities to use the streets for commercial lighting. He merely stated without comment the relator's contention to this effect. He pointed out that it had been held that the generation of electric current constitutes manufacturing, but he did not discuss whether the power to generate current carried with it the

[1] "The affidavit and answer of the defendant Edison Company puts in issue various allegations of the petition, and in addition sets out at considerable length facts upon which it bases its contention that the petition should be denied. Many of these facts are denied in the replying affidavits submitted on behalf of the relator and the corporation counsel. . . . In view, therefore, of the importance of the questions involved and of the issues of fact which are raised by the pleadings, an alternative writ should issue to determine all disputed questions of fact between the parties." *New York Law Journal*, July 26, 1917, p. 1413.

implied power to distribute this current. He found that the arguments were unsound which were presented by the company to support the claim that franchises had been granted by acquiescence or estoppel. His opinion, in part, was as follows: [1]

The contention of the relator is based upon the fact that the defendant Edison Company was incorporated pursuant to chapter 40 of the Laws of 1848, known as the Manufacturing Act, and that neither by that act nor any act amendatory thereof or supplemental thereto did that company acquire a franchise to use the public streets for private gain in carrying on a commercial business therein; and, further, that not having received any franchise from the state for that purpose, the Common Council of the former City of Brooklyn could not and did not legally grant any right to the said company to use the streets, avenues and public places of the city to carry on its business; and, further, that the same disability attaches to the incorporation of the Citizens, Municipal and Kings County Electric Light and Power companies. The defendant Edison Company was incorporated in 1887 [2] under the Act of 1848, which authorizes the formation of companies "for the purpose of carrying on any kind of manufacturing, mining, mechanical or chemical business." It has been held that the generation of electric current constitutes manufacturing.[3] . . . The certificate of incorporation of the Edison Company provided that the objects of the company were "to manufacture, use and sell electricity and electrical and mechanical apparatus in the City of Brooklyn for producing light, heat and power." It seems to be conceded that there was no other law in force at that time under which a company organized to manufacture

1 *The New York Law Journal*, July 26, 1917, p. 1413.

2 By error *The New York Law Journal* uses 1867 here.

3 Brush Electric Manufacturing Company *v.* Wemple, 129 N. Y. 543 (1892); Edison Electric Illuminating Company of New York *v.* Wemple, 129 N. Y. 665 (1892); Same *v.* Same, 141 N. Y. 471 (1894).

electricity for light, heat and power could have been incorporated in Brooklyn or Kings County, for Brooklyn and Kings County were expressly exempted from the operation of chapter 512 of the Laws of 1879, as amended by chapter 73 of the Laws of 1882,[1] which authorized any gas company incorporated under chapter 37 of the Laws of 1848, and "any corporation duly organized under the laws of this state for manufacturing and using electricity for producing light, heat or power," to use electricity for lighting public places and private dwellings in cities, villages and towns within the State. Why Brooklyn and Kings County should have been selected out of the whole state for exemption from this act is not apparent. It is possible that the Legislature may have been under the impression that the city of Brooklyn possessed the power to grant a franchise for that purpose, but there is nothing in the papers which have been submitted which clearly and conclusively points to the power of the City of Brooklyn to grant such a franchise. An examination of the charters of the City of Brooklyn of 1873 and of 1888, and of the amendments thereof down to the time of consolidation, does not disclose any power conferred upon the common council to grant franchises for supplying electric light, heat or power. Doubtless the Common Council of the City of Brooklyn did possess under its power to "regulate all matters connected with the public wharves and all business conducted thereon, and with all parks, places and streets of the city" (Laws of 1873, chap. 863, title 2, sec. 13, subdiv. 4), power to provide by ordinance for the lighting of the public streets of the city, such lighting being an incident to the use of the streets as public highways for the protection and safety of the public right of traveling over the highway. . . . . Such a use is for a street purpose distinguished from a municipal purpose. A street purpose is exclusively a highway purpose, and any use of the street which improves or benefits it as a highway is a proper street use. . . . Under the rules laid down by these cases, the right of the Common Council of Brooklyn, therefore, to contract with the Edi-

[1] By error *The New York Law Journal* uses 1862 here.

son Company or with any other corporation or person to furnish light in the streets under a *contract* would appear to have existed. This, however, would not confer upon the company the right to furnish light, heat or power to abutting owners for profit; in other words, it would not be broad enough to confer a franchise of that sort upon the defendant Edison Company.

Parenthetically, it is of interest to note that Mr. Justice Benedict took cognizance of the significance of earlier litigation in its bearing upon the right of the Edison Company to operate in the borough of Brooklyn, namely, the proceedings instituted by the Amsterdam Company and the Edison Company to enjoin the board of estimate and apportionment from revoking the franchise granted by the common council of the city of Brooklyn on December 30, 1895, to the State Company: [1]

The complaint of the Edison Company was dismissed upon the ground that its relationship to the Amsterdam Company was merely that of a stockholder and that it failed to prove that it leased the franchise of the Amsterdam Company or operated under it in any way. I understand that an appeal has been or is about to be taken from that judgment, and if the judgment dismissing the Edison Company's complaint should be reversed, then the question of the right of the Edison Company to maintain poles and wires in the Thirtieth Ward would again come directly in issue in that action.

Another attempt to move against the Edison Company on precisely the same grounds was made in 1917 by Henry Smith, a resident of ward 26 of the borough of Brooklyn. Mr. Justice Scudder granted a preliminary injunction on August 9, 1917, but vacated it some weeks later. Smith did not prosecute the action. The opinion rendered by Mr.

[1] Clements *v.* Edison Company, *The New York Law Journal*, July 26, 1917.

Justice Scudder, however, in vacating the injunction is of significance because of his statement about the company's "unlawful business" and of his approving comment on Mr. Justice Benedict's opinion.[1]

It seems to me that the preliminary injunction granted by me herein *ex-parte* should be vacated upon the ground that such injunction is unnecessary to the protection of plaintiff's personal or private rights to use the streets pending the trial of the action. I am unwilling to modify the injunction so as to allow the city officials to issue temporary permits to the defendant company to open the streets. If the defendant company has no franchise to use the streets to carry on its general business of electric lighting (and I concur in the recent opinion of Mr. Justice Benedict in People, etc. *v.* Williams, Law Journal, July 26, 1917, that it has not), it is illegal and wrongful for the city officials to issue any permit whatever to enable said defendant to conduct its unlawful business.

Tangled as is the skein of litigation bearing upon the question of validity of franchises, the city of New York is evincing no hesitancy in tracing the threads to what it believes to be their proper end. The recent petition of the Kings County Company to merge into and with itself the Edison Company brings out clearly the city's interpretation of actual and contemplated effects of recent and pending litigation regarding the validity of franchises in the borough of Brooklyn.[2]

[1] The vacating of the preliminary injunction of Mr. Justice Scudder as reported in *The New York Law Journal*, August 30, 1917.

[2] It was disclosed at the merger hearings that the board of estimate and apportionment passed a resolution that "the Corporation Counsel be and hereby is directed to petition the Attorney General of the State of New York to institute an action to forfeit the franchise of the Amsterdam Electric Light, Heat and Power Company on the ground of non-user." *Minutes of board of estimate and apportionment*, March 10, 1916, pp. 1397-1400.

In the month of December, 1918, hearings were conducted before the public service commission with regard to the petition of the Kings County Company for permission to merge and to execute a general mortgage upon plant and property. The Kings County Company acquired in November, 1898, the entire capital stock of the Edison Company, but according to the terms of a lease the latter company has since 1899 been operating the properties of the two companies as one system and paying over all the net profits of the business to the Kings Company. The city of New York entered strong protest against the contemplated merger: [1]

The Corporation Counsel of the City of New York appearing herein for and on behalf of said City, herewith presents to the Commission the formal and earnest objections to the granting of the orders prayed for herein. The grounds for such objections are hereinafter set forth at length. In a general way these grounds are the following:

1. That the petitioner, Kings County Electric Light and Power Company, is not possessed either through its incorporation under Chapter 40, Laws of 1848, or through any grant from the local authorities of the former City of Brooklyn or the present City of New York, of any valid franchise or right to construct, maintain or operate electrical conductors for light, heat and power purposes in or through the streets and highways in the Borough of Brooklyn.

2. That the Edison Electric Illuminating Company of Brooklyn to the merger of which by the Kings County Electric Light and Power Company, the approval of your Commission is asked, does not possess, either through its incorporation under Chapter 40 of the Laws of 1848, or through any grant from the local authorities of the former City of Brooklyn or the present City of New York, any valid franchise or right to construct, maintain or operate electrical conductors for light,

[1] *Answer of the City of New York*, pp. 1-4.

heat and power purposes in or through the streets and highways in the Borough of Brooklyn.

3. That said Edison Electric Illuminating Company has never acquired nor does it now possess by its consolidation with or merger of any other corporation or by lease, assignment or transfer from any other corporation, any franchise or right to construct, maintain or operate electrical conductors for light, heat or power purposes in or through the streets and highways in the Borough of Brooklyn.

4. That any consent, approval or order granted or made at this time on the above petitions, would be a recognition by your Commission of valid franchise rights and would work serious and permanent injury to the City of New York and to the citizens and residents thereof, by reason of the fact that litigation is now pending and undetermined wherein the City and residents of the Borough of Brooklyn are seeking to have established the invalidity of the franchises now claimed and exercised by these companies.

5. That your petitioner, the Kings County Electric Light and Power Company, is not properly organized to exercise the rights or franchises of an electric light corporation. It is a business corporation organized and existing under the Manufacturing Corporations Act of 1848 (Chapter 40, Laws of 1848), and for this reason cannot, under the existing provisions of law, acquire the legal right to construct, maintain or operate electrical conductors in the streets. . . .

6. That the approval of your Commission to the issuance of the six million dollars of bonds and to the execution of the proposed mortgage or deed of trust, which is intended to stand as security for bonds to the enormous amount of one hundred million dollars, would be unwarranted and inadvisable, in view of the questions raised by the City as to the invalidity of the Company's franchise. The investing public relies on, and has a right to rely on, the integrity of securities issued with the sanction of your Commission, and, having this in mind, it need hardly be suggested to the Commission that the questions raised by the City deserve close examination and careful con-

sideration before any steps are taken under the present application.

Commissioner Hervey inquired whether the assistant corporation counsel who appeared for the city believed that the Kings County Company would obtain some rights by the proposed merger. He received an affirmative answer, supplemented by the explanation that if the city could proceed separately against the charter of the Edison Company as well as against the special franchise, it would be in a more favorable position than if it had to act after the Edison Company was merged into the Kings County Company.[1] In the same connection, the assistant corporation counsel voiced the hopes of the city regarding the results of appeals pending and the fears of the city entertained with respect to the contemplated merger:[2]

. . . There is an appeal pending by the City, and an appeal also pending by the Company, from this judgment entered upon the Referee's report; and it may be that the Appellate Division in this litigation will pass upon the franchise of the Edison Company in Brooklyn, which the Referee refused to do; and it may be that we will have, and we expect to have, an opinion in the Appellate Division holding that the Edison Company is without a franchise in the Borough of Brooklyn. So in that way this Amsterdam litigation has disclosed this cloud, which really involves the Edison Company's franchise and is material here. . . . A merger of this company [the Edison Company] will destroy this joint plaintiff [the Amsterdam Company and the Edison Company], and what could we do in the Appellate Division? The plaintiff is gone and we are appealing from the judgment. . . . That brings me to the question not only of that litigation, but of the matter of the application to the Attorney General. . . . We can proceed against

[1] *Minutes of hearings*, case no. 2351, December 16, 1918, p. 9.

[2] *Minutes of hearings*, case no. 2351, December 23, 1918, pp. 168-170.

the company, and we can show the standing of the company, but it seems to me if this company goes out of existence—and the Court of Appeals has held that where there is a merger the company absolutely goes out of existence — we cannot complain that this company is a manufacturing company; and, moreover, the new company can go ahead operating. The merger will take place not under the Stock Corporation Law applicable to business corporations, which would be applicable to manufacturing corporations, but it would take place under the special provisions applicable to public service corporations, and the result would be a public service corporation that you would have there. We would have to fight a public service corporation and not a manufacturing corporation.

Chairman of the meeting: "Up to the present time you are contending that you are fighting a body which has not a legal existence."

Assistant corporation counsel: "That is the idea."

Chairman: "And which, to exercise the rights it now claims, ought to have a legal existence; whereas, as the result of the merger, it will assume a legal existence and then be able to exercise its rights lawfully."

Counsel: "Yes, certainly; will thereafter be able to exercise its rights and exercise its franchise lawfully." [1]

The attorney representing the interests of the companies inquired in what way the corporate life or capacity of two manufacturing corporations could become so enriched through the merging of the companies that a different kind of corporation would result. The assistant corporation counsel answered that this result could be brought about through the "necromancy of law," the "statutory legerdemain" of these corporations.[2]

It is difficult to see what rights the city could lose through the merger. The action of the public service commission

[1] *Minutes of hearings*, case no. 2351, December 23, 1918, p. 170.

[2] *Ibid.*, p. 171.

in granting permission to merge could scarcely be conceived as having the power of changing the status of the franchises held by the companies that obtained the permission. However, the public service commissioners, in deference to the city's fears or in abundance of caution, inserted the following provision in their order approving the merger: [1]

The permission and approval of the Commission to the said merger shall not be construed to revive or validate any lapsed or invalid franchise or to enlarge or add to the powers and privileges contained in the grant of any franchise or to waive any forfeiture, or to affect the rights or remedies of any party in any action or proceeding now pending to which the Kings County Electric Light and Power Company (now Brooklyn Edison Company, Inc.), the Edison Electric Illuminating Company of Brooklyn, or any person or corporation under whom they or either of them may claim to be a party.

The public service commission did not subscribe to the broad statement that neither of the two companies was a public service corporation. Instead, the commissioners held that each of the companies came under the definition of an "electrical corporation," as given in the public service commissions law: [2]

The term "electrical corporation," when used in this chapter, includes every corporation, company, association, joint-stock association, partnership and person, their lessees, trustees or receivers appointed by any court whatsoever (other than a railroad or street railroad corporation generating electricity solely for railroad or street railroad purposes or for the use of its tenants and not for sale to others) owning, operating, or

[1] Case no. 2351, *Order approving merger and consenting to mortgage*, p. 2.

[2] Subdivision 13, section 2. Cited by Commissioner Kracke in memorandum upon granting of application to merge, pp. 3, 4.

managing any electric plant except where electricity is generated or distributed by the producer solely on or through private property for railroad or street railroad purposes or for its own use or for the use of its tenants and not for sale to others.

The public service commissions law defined the term "electric plant": [1]

The term "electric plant," when used in this chapter, includes all real estate, fixtures and personal property operated, owned, or to be used for or in connection with or to facilitate the generation, transmission, distribution, sale or furnishing of electricity for light, heat or power; and any conduits, ducts or other devices, materials, apparatus or property for containing, holding or carrying conductors used or to be used for the transmission of electricity for light, heat or power.

Another statute to be considered in connection with the organization of electrical corporations is the transportation corporations act of 1890,[2] entitled "An act in relation to transportation corporations, excepting railroads, constituting chapter forty of the general laws." Article VI treated of gas and electrical corporations. Section sixty provided: [3]

Three or more persons may become a corporation for manu-

[1] Subdivision 12, section 2.

[2] Laws of 1890, ch. 566.

[3] Section 60 of chapter 566 of the laws of 1890 was amended by section 1 of chapter 575 of the laws of 1900 to read:

"Three or more persons may become a corporation for manufacturing and supplying gas for lighting the streets and public and private buildings of cities, villages and towns in this state, or for manufacturing and using electricity for producing light, heat or power, and in lighting streets, avenues, public parks and places, and public and private buildings of cities, villages and towns within this state, or for two or more of such purposes . . . the term of its existence not to exceed fifty years."

facturing and supplying gas for lighting the streets and public and private buildings of any city, village or town, or two or more villages or towns not over five miles distant from each other, in this state, or for manufacturing and using electricity for producing light, heat or power, and in lighting streets, avenues, public parks and places, and public and private buildings of cities, villages and towns within this state, ... the term of its existence not to exceed fifty years. . . . .

Subdivision two of section sixty-one gave the following additional powers: [1]

If incorporated for the purpose of using electricity for light, heat or power, to carry on the business of lighting by electricity or using it for heat or power in cities, towns and villages within this state, and the streets, avenues, public parks and places thereof, and public and private dwellings therein; and for the purposes of such business to generate and supply electricity; and to make, sell or lease all machines, instruments, apparatus and other equipments therefor, and to lay, erect and construct suitable wires or other conductors, with the necessary poles, pipes or other fixtures in, on, over and under the streets, avenues, public parks and places of such cities, towns or villages, for conducting and distributing electricity, with the consent of the municipal authorities thereof, and in such manner and under such reasonable regulations as they may prescribe.

Subdivision three of section sixty-one provided:

Any two or more corporations organized under this article or under any general or special law of the state for the purpose of

[1] Laws of 1890, ch. 566, section 61, subdivision 2. Another paragraph was added to this subdivision by the laws of 1909, ch. 219:

"Any electric light company in any town or village in this state having a contract with any town or incorporated village for the lighting of streets, parks, squares or public buildings in any town or village, shall have the right and is hereby vested with the power and authority to acquire such real estate as may be necessary for the purposes of its incorporation."

carrying on any business which a corporation organized under this article might carry on, may consolidate such corporations into a single corporation by complying with the provisions of the business corporations law relating to the consolidation of business corporations.[1]

Section sixty-five laid upon " any electric-light corporation " the obligation, under certain conditions, of supplying electric light on application.[2] Section sixty-six permitted " every gas light and electric light corporation " to require of the consumer a deposit of a sum of money as a condition of furnishing light.[3] Section sixty-seven set forth the circumstances under which agents of " any gas light or electric light corporation " might enter buildings to examine meters, lights, and lighting appliances in general.[4]

[1] Laws of 1890, ch. 566, section 61, subdivision 3. In the laws of 1909, ch. 219, subdivision 3 of section 61 reads:

" Subject to the permission and approval of the proper public service commission, any two or more corporations organized under this article or under any general or special law of this state for the purpose of carrying on any business which a corporation organized under this article might carry on, may consolidate such corporations into a single corporation, and any such corporation may with the like permission and approval be merged with any other such corporation, upon complying with the provisions of the business corporations law relating to the consolidation of business corporations, and the stock corporations law relating to the merger of stock corporations."

A fourth subdivision was added to section 61 of chapter 566 of the laws of 1890 by the laws of 1899 (Laws of 1899, ch. 565, section 61, subdivision 4). It provided:

"Any corporation organized under this article or under any general or special law of this state for the purpose of using electricity for light, heat or power in cities, other than of the first class towns or villages within this state, may . . acquire the . . power of supplying steam to consumers from . . stations through pipes laid in the public streets . . with the consent of the municipal authorities thereof . . . "

[2] Laws of 1890, ch. 566, section 65.

[3] *Ibid.*, section 66.

[4] *Ibid.*, section 67.

The "saving clause" in the transportation corporations law provided: [1]

The repeal of any law or any part of it specified in the annexed schedule shall not affect or impair any act done, or right accruing, or accrued or acquired, or liability, penalty, forfeiture or punishment incurred prior to May first, 1891, under or by virtue of any law so repealed, but the same may be asserted, enforced, prosecuted or inflicted, as fully and to the same extent, as if such law had not been repealed. . . .

The "construction" clause stated: [2]

The provisions of this chapter, so far as they are substantially the same as those of laws existing on April 30th, 1891, shall be construed as a continuation of such laws, modified or amended according to the language employed in this chapter and not as new enactments; and references in laws not repealed to provisions of laws incorporated into this chapter and repealed shall be construed as applying to the provisions so incorporated, and nothing in this chapter shall be construed to amend or repeal any provision of the Criminal or Penal Code.

The transportation corporations law of 1890 repealed all of chapter 37 of the laws of 1848; [3] and all of chapter 512 of the laws of 1879.[4] In the schedule of laws repealed by

[1] Laws of 1890, chapter 566, article 10, section 161.

[2] Laws of 1890, chapter 566, article 10, section 162.

[3] Chapter 563 of the laws of 1890 had repealed sections 4, 7, 9, and 23 of chapter 37 of the laws of 1848; and chapter 564 of the laws of 1890 had repealed sections 3, 5, 6, 8, 10 to 17 inclusive, and 20 to 22 inclusive. The transportation corporations law of 1892 (Laws of 1892, ch. 617) again repealed all of chapter 37 of the laws of 1848, as did chapter 687 of the laws of 1892.

[4] Chapter 617 of the laws of 1892, amending the transportation corporations law of 1890, repealed all of chapter 512 of the laws of 1879; and all of it was again repealed by chapter 687 of the laws of the same year, 1892. In the schedule of laws repealed by the transportation corporations law of 1909, (L. 1909, ch. 219), all of chapter 512 of the laws of 1879 was again repealed.

the transportation corporations act of 1909, all of chapter 73 of the laws of 1882 was repealed.[1] The general manufacturing corporations act (Laws of 1848, chapter 40) consisted of twenty-seven sections. In the series of general laws passed in 1890 all the sections were repealed;[2] and in the schedule of laws repealed by chapter 687 of the laws of 1892, the general manufacturing corporations act as a whole was repealed.

The effect of incorporation of the Edison and Kings County companies under the general manufacturing corporations act, viewed apart from other statutory enactments, will next be considered. If it were conceded that the common council of the city of Brooklyn had the power to grant local franchises for public and private lighting under the charters of 1873 and of 1888 and their amendments, it would appear that the companies might fairly claim the right to operate under the manufacturing act without any further state legislation. If, as has been said, a corporation generating electric current is engaged in manufacturing, a company might properly be organized under the manufacturing act for the manufacture of electricity. It was probably taken for granted by the companies that the general permission to generate electric current carried with it the general state permission to distribute the current. Otherwise, the right of a company contemplating making use of the generating current by selling it to private and public consumers would be but a barren right. That the Edison Company considered that the power to generate carried with it the implied power to distribute seems ap-

[1] Chapter 73 of the laws of 1882 had been repealed by chapter 687 of the laws of 1892.

[2] Chapter 563 repealed sections 4, 7, 9 and 26; chapter 564 repealed sections 3, 5, 6, 8, 10 to 25 inclusive, and 27; chapter 567 repealed sections 1 and 2.

parent from its certificate of incorporation, in which the objects for which the company was formed were said to be "to manufacture, use and sell electricity, and electrical and mechanical apparatus in the city of Brooklyn for producing light, heat and power." This view depends ultimately for its strength upon whether the common council of the city of Brooklyn had the power to grant the special franchises under which the companies occupied the streets in the pursuit of commercial lighting.

The manufacturing act of 1848 does not stand by itself, however. Its relation to the acts of 1879 and 1882 [1] is a question of practical importance. The third section of the act of 1879 expressly exempted the city of Brooklyn and the county of Kings from the provisions of the act, authorizing any corporation organized under the gas-light act of 1848 [2] to use electricity instead of gas. The act of 1882 amended section one of the law of 1879 so as to confer authority to use electricity instead of gas, not only upon companies organized under the gas-light act of 1848, but upon "any corporation duly organized under the laws of this state for manufacturing and using electricity for producing light, heat or power"—a corporation, for example, organized under the manufacturing corporations act. The third section of the act of 1879 was not amended. Apparently, therefore, the act of 1882 left intact the exemption clause in the act of 1879.

If this construction be correct, it must be conceded that any provision in the Brooklyn charter of 1888, though subsequent in point of enactment, must needs be specific in the authority conferred upon the common council to act at variance with the initial disability imposed upon the city by reason of its exclusion from the acts of 1879 and 1882. A

[1] Chapters 512 and 73 respectively.

[2] Laws of 1848, ch. 37.

special act, like a city charter, cannot be held to repeal a provision of a general law, like the laws of 1879 and 1882, unless the conflict be unmistakable. Had the Brooklyn charter of 1888 expressly authorized the council to grant a special franchise to any corporation organized under the laws of New York for manufacturing electricity, there could be little question that such a provision would be construed as a repeal of the section which excluded Brooklyn from the law of 1879. It is quite otherwise with a general charter provision conferring the customary control over streets. Nevertheless, the common council acted on the assumption that there was vested in them the authority to grant these franchises. Moreover, when a bill passed the legislature granting direct authority to the Edison Company to open the streets of the city of Brooklyn and maintain electrical conductors therein, the governor vetoed the bill on the ground that it infringed upon the franchise-granting authority of the mayor and common council of the city.[1] Subsequently, October 29, 1888, the common council granted to the Edison Company the franchise. The governor's opinion with reference to the power and authority of the common council of Brooklyn to grant the franchise which the Edison Company sought was not necessarily based upon expert knowledge of the law. It may have been merely a manifestation of his support of the principle of local self-government. It is of interest, but it is not of controlling weight.

It is also of interest that the secretary of state filed the companies' certificates of incorporation without protest. If the act of 1879 as amended in 1882 did not permit the city of Brooklyn to obtain the services of companies which, being organized under the manufacturing act of 1848, were

[1] *Brief of the Edison Company*, p. 31.

"duly organized under the laws of this state for manufacturing and using electricity for producing light, heat and power," the companies should not have been allowed to file their certificates of incorporation. The Edison Company commented upon the filing of the certificates of incorporation as follows:[1]

> The corporations at the time of their incorporation claimed the right to exercise the powers conferred by the amendment of 1882 and the act was practically construed to that end. The certificate of incorporation of the Citizens Company, executed December 6, 1883, states the objects of the incorporation in the precise language of the amendment, to wit:
>
> "That the objects for which said Company is to be formed are manufacturing and using electricity for producing light, heat or power and using electricity as a means of lighting streets, avenues, public parks and places, and public and private dwellings of cities, villages and towns within this State. . . . That the name of the city and county in which the operations of said Company are to be carried on is the City of Brooklyn, County of Kings and State of New York. . . ."
>
> The certificates of the other companies, while not conforming so closely to the language employed in the statute, indicate nevertheless clearly that their respective objects are to carry on an electric business in the City of Brooklyn, County of Kings. . . . These certificates were accepted by the Secretary of State and filed. It would have been his duty to reject them had it not been considered that the existing legislation authorized the formation of electric corporations in the then City of Brooklyn.

One of the arguments presented by the Edison Company[2] developed the claim that the amendment of 1882 "is so all-inclusive both as to the corporations whose powers

[1] *Brief of the Edison Company*, pp. 28, 29. The companies referred to are the Edison, Kings County, Municipal, and Citizens companies.

[2] *Brief of the Edison Company*, p. 25.

are declared and the cities and towns to which it referred that its meaning and effect cannot be restricted by Section 3 of the act amended." This argument encounters the obvious rejoinder that if the legislature had intended to extend the benefit of the act to the whole state, it could readily have expressed that intention by repealing section 3 of the act of 1879. On the other hand, it does seem strange that the legislature should have deliberately singled out the city of Brooklyn to deny it the benefits of commercial electric lighting which every other city in the state could enjoy. It may be that failure to repeal the Brooklyn exemption was due to carelessness or to some erroneous assumption as to the state of the law.

The argument has been advanced that the Edison Company "has express power and authority under the Transportation Corporations Law to carry on the business of manufacturing and distributing electricity in the Borough of Brooklyn under the franchises granted to it and its merged and affiliated companies."[1] The essence of this argument is as follows:[2]

> Questions relating to the right of the Companies to conduct the business of supplying electricity for public and private use under laws existing prior to the effective date of the Transportation Corporations Law are now of little . . . practical importance. All prior acts relating to such corporations were repealed by the revision of laws as effected through the enactment of the Transportation Corporations Law and other general incorporation laws. It is expressly provided that the provisions of the Transportation Corporations Law relating to gas and electric corporations are a continuation of all prior laws relating to such corporations, modified or amended according to the language employed by the Transportation Corporations Law.

[1] *Brief of Edison Company*, p. 18.

[2] *Ibid.*, p. 34.

According to the rule laid down by the legislature in the construction clause [1] of the transportation corporations law of 1890,[2] it is clear that this statute did bring about a measure of continuation of prior laws. By this clause, however, prior laws are continued only so far as the provisions of the transportation corporations law " are *substantially the same* " as those of existing laws. It is difficult to see what support can be claimed from this provision by the companies affected by the exemption clause in the act of 1879. To be sure, this law was included in the schedule of laws repealed by the transportation corporations law of 1890, and the amending law of 1882 was specifically repealed later.[3] But the companies affected by the exemption clause in the act of 1879 were not released from the limitations because of the repeal of the act itself. The " saving clause " [4] of the transportation corporations act provided that " the repeal of any law . . . shall not affect or impair any . . . right accruing, accrued or acquired . . . by virtue of any law so repealed." But if a company could not have acquired its right to operate under the repealed laws, how can it claim that it was advantageously affected either by the continuation of statutory provisions " substantially the same " or by the repeal of laws under which it had acquired no right? The act did not purport to cure irregularities or to create legal rights where none existed at the time.

[1] *Supra*, p. 123.

[2] Laws of 1890, ch. 566, sec. 162. On page 36 of the brief of the Edison Company, attention is directed to the fact that the same provision as to construction was contained in Laws of 1890, ch. 563, sec. 25; Laws of 1890, ch. 564, sec. 72; Laws of 1892, ch. 617, sec. 162; Laws of 1892, ch. 687, sec. 63; and that it is "now contained in the General Construction Law and made applicable to all laws (L. 1909, Chap. 27, Section 95)."

[3] *Supra*, p. 124.

[4] *Supra*, p. 123.

It is claimed that certain provisions of the transportation corporations law show that it applies to all electric light companies whether these companies have been incorporated under it or under prior laws.[1] Thus "any electric light company" having the specified contracts is vested with the power to acquire real estate necessary for the purposes of its incorporation.[2] "Any two or more corporations organized under this article, or under any general or special law of this state . . ." are given certain permissions regarding consolidation and merging.[3] "Any corporation organized under this article or under any general or special law of this state . . ." may acquire, under specified conditions, the power of using the streets in supplying steam to consum-

[1] *Brief of the Edison Company*, pp. 38-40.

The brief of the Edison Company, p. 37, cites the case of the Municipal Gas Company *v.* Rice, 138 N. Y. 151 (1893) as an instance of litigation concerning the effect of the transportation corporations law upon corporations organized under prior laws, and gives a lengthy extract from the opinion of the court of appeals. A part of the extract herewith follows:

"It is quite plain . . . that the legislature, in adopting the revision, intended to permit such corporations to amend the certificate in such a way as to authorize them to exercise powers and to enlarge the purposes and objects of the corporation beyond the limit within which they were restricted before."

The company had been incorporated under chapter 37 of the laws of 1848. It sought to amend its certificate to enable it to manufacture and use electricity for producing light, heat and power. This meant that it was enlarging its powers, since it was originally incorporated as a gas company. The secretary of state refused to file the certificate, maintaining that section 60 of article 6, chapter 566 of the laws of 1890 (since amended; *supra*, p. 120) permitted incorporation either as a gas company or as an electric company but not as both, and that the one certificate of incorporation could not, therefore, include powers of both gas and electric lighting. The court upheld the company.

[2] Laws of 1909, ch. 219, sec. 61, subdiv. 2. *Supra*, note, p. 121.

[3] Laws of 1909, ch. 219, sec. 61, subdiv. 3. *Supra*, note, p. 122.

ers.[1] The obligation of supplying electric light is laid upon "any electric light corporation." [2] The privilege of requiring a deposit is granted to "every electric light corporation." [3] The provisions regarding the examination of meters and lighting appliances in general, refer to agents of "any electric light corporation." [4]

It may be that the Brooklyn companies acquired certain additional powers under these general provisions, but it is open to very grave doubt whether they could claim that such provisions operated to legalize their commercial activities if these had previously been illegally carried on. For example, let it be conceded that these companies were legally organized under the manufacturing act to manufacture electric current, and that they may, in consequence, be properly designated "electric light corporations;" it could scarcely be argued from this concession that an authorization to "every electric light corporation" to require a consumer's deposit implied that a company thereby received full power to use the streets for the distribution of current to consumers although it enjoyed no such power before.

Commenting upon the Edison Company's arguments regarding the doctrines of acquiescence and estoppel, Mr. Justice Benedict said: [5]

The argument based upon these facts that a franchise was granted to it by estoppel or acquiescence is unsound. People ex rel. Browning, King & Co. *v.* Stover (145 App. Div. 259, 262), where Scott, J., points out the distinction which exists in this respect between mandamus to compel public officials

[1] Laws of 1899, ch. 565, sec. 61, subdiv. 4. *Supra*, note, p. 122.

[2] Laws of 1890, ch. 566, sec. 65. *Supra*, note, p. 122.

[3] *Ibid.*, sec. 66. *Supra*, note, p. 122.

[4] *Ibid.*, sec. 67. *Supra*, note, p. 122.

[5] Clements *v.* Edison Company, *New York Law Journal*, July 26, 1917.

to perform their duty to remove street encroachments and an action in equity to enjoin a private right. The same defendant further contends that since it has been taxed yearly by the state on its franchise, that is a recognition by the state of the existence of the franchise and works an estoppel against the contrary contention. But this is not any more sound than the other proposition (see Holmes Elec. Protective Co. *v.* Armstrong, 97 Misc. 184, where Hotchkiss, J., discusses the question with care and precision, pp. 193-197).

One of the cases cited by the Edison Company [1] in support of the proposition that the right to exercise the special franchises had become vested in the company and was protected by the doctrine of estoppel, was the case of Wyandotte Electric Light Company *v.* City of Wyandotte.[2]

The Wyandotte Electric Light Company was incorporated on September 19, 1889, for the purpose of manufacturing and supplying electricity for light, heat and power. On the twenty-fifth day of the same month, it obtained a municipal franchise from the city of Wyandotte, Michigan. Extension of poles and wires and service was made by the company freely from that time on. The common council of the city of Wyandotte passed a resolution on August 3, 1898, to direct the removal of all unused wires, hoods and appliances; and on August 17, 1898, it adopted a resolution revoking all licenses or permissions which had been given by the common council to the company authorizing it to erect electrical apparatus in the streets for the purpose of carrying on its business. The resolution stated, further, that if the company desired to occupy the streets, it would have to obtain a franchise from the common council for that purpose. The company brought action to restrain the

[1] *Brief of the Edison Company*, p. 52.

[2] Wyandotte Electric Light Company *v.* City of Wyandotte, 124 Mich. 43 (1900).

city from interfering with the poles and wires. The defendant city answered by claiming the benefits of a cross-bill, and by maintaining that the common council was within its rights in revoking on August 17, 1898, the *license* granted by the council to the company on September 25, 1889, since the grant was merely a license, revocable at the will of the city. Decree was entered for the company. In its opinion, the court said:

> There is one controlling question in the case. Upon its determination depend the rights of the parties. It can, perhaps, be better stated by stating the several contentions. The defendants contend that complainant, by organizing under the general manufacturers' act, obtained no franchise direct from the legislature to use the streets and highways, such as it would have acquired under the electric light companies' act. Their second contention results from the first, namely, that the city had no authority to grant the franchises claimed by complainant.[1]

The company contended that since the state had recognized for nine years the validity of its incorporation, the state alone could complain; and that the city was estopped from claiming that the company ought to have been organized under another statute or that it was not qualified to exercise the franchise granting the authority to manufacture and sell electricity for the purpose of lighting.

In another part of the opinion the court stated:

> The purposes for which complainant was organized are precisely those covered by the electric-lighting act. It could not

[1] It was brought out in the case that at the time the Wyandotte Electric Light Company was organized under the chapter relating to the incorporation of manufacturing companies generally, there was in existence in Michigan a statute authorizing the organization of electric light companies.

carry on its proposed business without the use of the streets, and immediately applied to the city for such use. The city so understood it. . . . Whether the defendant city knew under what act complainant was organized does not appear. . . . . Whether the act under which it was organized would permit its incorporation, we need not determine. The State for nine years recognized its incorporation as valid. The defendant city dealt with it for the same time as a valid corporation, granted it the franchise as requested, permitted it to erect and maintain an expensive plant; and now, when the city has gone into the business of municipal and commercial lighting, seeks to crush it, to utterly destroy its property, and compel its patrons to become the patrons of the city, which charges more for its service than does complainant. It is needless to say that the defendants are without equity, and that their contention ought not to prevail if the courts of equity have the power to prevent it.

It remains to be seen whether the higher courts will sustain the movement to invalidate the franchises of the Edison system through the interposition of technicalities, as in the instance of the Amsterdam franchise,[1] or through interpretation of the manufacturing corporations act of 1848 and the special acts of 1879 and 1882, with regard to the Edison, Kings County, Municipal and Citizens franchises.[2] It

[1] *Supra*, pp. 103-107.

[2] As has been indicated, (*Supra*, pp. 100-102), the Municipal and Citizens companies were not original grantees of the franchises which were transferred to the Edison Company with the merger of these two companies into the latter company. Concerning these franchises, the corporation counsel said:

"The grants made by the Common Council to Charles Cooper and Company and Pope, Sewall and Company referred to above may be said to have been invalid for the reason that they were granted to individuals who had acquired no franchise from the State and because the Common Council had no power to grant them. The invalidity of these grants could not have been cured by their subsequent acquirement by the Municipal Electric Light Company and the Citizens

is likely that it would not be difficult to find technical points of omission and commission in the records concerning many franchises that would turn out to be not in strict accord with the terms of the original franchise instruments. These would need to be considered in the light of later agreements of the companies with the city. What might seem at first to be violation of an original agreement, would turn out perhaps to be only an irregularity waived by the city through a series of acts.[1] It is probable that years of occupancy of the streets by the company will constitute a fact receiving much attention by the courts.

The four remaining franchises of the system of what is now the Brooklyn Edison Company, Inc., fall under the same general attack, since the four companies were all organized under the general manufacturing corporations act. No amount of argument concerning the acts of 1848, 1879, and 1882 can hide, however, the fundamental fact that both the former city of Brooklyn and the present borough of Brooklyn accepted the services of the companies, allowed extensions, permitted heavy investments, and gave every evidence of accepting unquestioningly the right of these companies to operate. If it was the deliberate legislative intent to shut out the city of Brooklyn and the county of Kings from the privileges accorded the cities, towns, and villages throughout the rest of the state, the acts of 1879 and 1882 [2] require no subtle construction. Rather, it becomes difficult to understand why such a determined plan was not carried out in some way by its instigators to the

Electric Illuminating Company. Both of these corporations were formed under the Manufacturing Corporations Act, Chapter 40 of the Laws of 1848, the former on August 2, 1884 and the latter on December 13, 1883." *Answer of the city of New York*, p. 11.

[1] *Supra*, p. 105.

[2] Chapters 512 and 73 respectively.

extent of actually suppressing those privileges; for we can hardly attribute to the legislatures of 1879 and 1882 the veiled intention of desiring companies to enter illegally upon the pursuit of the business of commercial electric lighting in the city of Brooklyn. If the legislature was merely under the impression that the common council of the city of Brooklyn had the authority under the city charter to grant the franchises to the electric companies, the acts of 1879 and 1882 take on a harmless appearance as far as the city of Brooklyn was concerned in its desire to obtain electric lighting for public and private purposes. What caused the acquiescence on all sides in the granting of the franchises and the operation of the companies, if the granting was unwarranted and the operation illegal? What attitude the higher courts will take remains to be seen.

How many other franchises held by the electric lighting companies of New York City are connected with the manufacturing corporations act will be noted in passing. Of the five franchises claimed by the New York Edison Company, three came down through original grantees incorporated under the manufacturing corporations act: the East River Electric Light, Harlem Lighting, and the North New York Lighting companies. Two of the three original grantees of franchises directly or indirectly controlled by the United Electric Light and Power Company were incorporated under this act, namely, the Brush Electric Illuminating Company of New York, and the Ball Electrical Illuminating Company. The original grantee of the one franchise of the Long Acre Electric Light and Power Company was the American Electric Manufacturing Company, incorporated under the manufacturing act; and the American Electric Illuminating Company, to which the franchise was later transferred, was also incorporated under this act. The Pelham Bay Park Electric Light, Power and Storage Company and the Eastchester Electric Company, original grantees of six franchises now claimed by the Westchester Lighting Company for electric light operations in the city of New York, were incorporated under this act. The only franchise, therefore, which the Westchester Lighting Company has for its first district operations, not connected with the general manufacturing corporations act, is the one granted to the Pelham Electric Light and Power Company. Five of the sixteen franchises now held by the New York and Queens Electric Light and Power Company came down from the original grantee, the Flushing Electric Light and Power Company, incorporated under this act. The United Electric Light and Power Company received its present name on December 9, 1889. It had been called the Safety Electric Light and Power Company. This Safety Electric Light and Power Company was incorporated under the manufacturing act.

It does not seem at all likely that the validity of these franchises can be assailed because of any connection which they have with the general manufacturing corporations act of 1848. Chapter 73 of the laws of 1882 is virtually meaningless if it does not extend to those companies organized under the manufacturing act [1] the same authority which it specifically extends to the corporations organized under the gas act.[2]

An interesting suggestion of the possibility of questioning the validity of franchises obtained by original grantees incorporated under the general manufacturing corporations law is found in the case of Public Service Commission,

[1] This statement must be qualified by the obvious reminder that the companies organized under the manufacturing act, but operating in the former city of Brooklyn, meet the disability alleged to result from the exemption clause in the 1879 act.

[2] *Supra*, p. 108.

Second District, *v.* J. and J. Rogers Company. The public service commission for the second district brought action for an injunction [1] against the J. and J. Rogers Company, to restrain the company from distributing electricity for light, heat and power in the town of Jay or "in that part of the town known as Ausable Forks." The petition alleged that the company was a manufacturing corporation without authority from the town board to occupy the streets of the town of Jay, and without permission from the public service commission to exercise any franchise. The petition alleged further that the company was "without corporate capacity to receive or exercise a franchise from the town of Jay for the purpose of transmitting and distributing electricity to the public generally," and was "disqualified to be permitted to transmit or distribute electricity as a public service corporation by the petitioner, not having been incorporated under the Transportation Corporations Law." [2] In delivering the opinion of the court, Mr. Justice Rudd said:

The defendant admits that it has transmitted and distributed electricity to householders for lighting, collecting for such

[1] Public Service Commission, Second District, *v.* J. and J. Rogers Company, 103 N. Y. Misc. 711 (1918).

[2] The commission stated that the J. and J. Rogers Company was originally incorporated in January, 1871, as J. and J. Rogers Iron Company under the manufacturing corporations law of 1848; and that in June, 1893, "the defendant was reorganized under the corporate name of J. and J. Rogers Company by filing in the office of the secretary of state pursuant to the provisions of the stock corporation law a reorganization agreement and certificate. The defendant has never been reorganized or incorporated under the transportation corporations law." The J. and J. Rogers Company is engaged in the manufacture of sulphite and ground wood pulp and paper. In 1897 the company installed a lighting plant for its own use; and it erected, later, a power plant generating electricity for both power and lighting purposes. Subsequently, it undertook commercial lighting.

service annually about $2,700, and that no express franchise has been granted to the defendant by the town authorities of the town of Jay; that the transmission of electric current by the defendant is by means of a line or lines of poles and wires partly located in the public highway; that the defendant is a corporation organized as a manufacturing company and that it has never been incorporated under the Transportation Corporations Law; that the entire business of the defendant, including generation of electricity and manufacturing, amounts approximately to the sum of $1,080,000 gross each year.

The court summed up the contention of the company as follows:

The contention of the defendant is that the court is without jurisdiction, that this is a proceeding brought under section 74 of the Public Service Commission Law,[1] and because that section specifically relates to gas corporations and electric corporations and the regulation of the price of gas and electricity, defendant not being either a gas or electric corporation, that therefore the court cannot, under the petition, restrain the defendant.

The court added:

There does not seem to be much force in this contention. It

[1] Section 74 of the Public Service Commissions Law, to which the court referred, reads as follows:

"Whenever either commission shall be of the opinion that a gas corporation, electric corporation or municipality within its jurisdiction is failing or omitting or about to fail or omit to do anything required of it by law or by order of the commission or is doing anything or about to do anything or permitting anything or about to permit anything to be done, contrary to or in violation of law or of any order of the commission, it shall direct counsel to the commission to commence an action or proceeding in the Supreme Court of the State of New York in the name of the commission for the purpose of having such violations or threatened violations stopped and prevented either by mandamus or injunction."

is a manufacturing company, it does generate and furnish electric power for heating and light. . . . The question is simply this: Can a manufacturing corporation, organized as such, and doing business as such in large volume, assume in a small way to do an electrical business which is in violation, not only of the spirit, but the very terms, of the statutes. If it is a manufacturing corporation, it cannot do an electrical business. If it is an electrical corporation, as above stated, organized for that purpose, it cannot begin to transact business until its application meets with the approval of the Public Service Commission. By a violation of the law it has not secured an implied franchise.

From the decree of the court granting the injunction prayed for, the company appealed. The case was brought before the appellate division of the supreme court, third department.[1] Mr. Justice Woodward affirmed the judgment of the lower court, but modified the injunction by providing that it should not be construed "to enjoin the defendant from conveying electricity from its own generating plant across the public streets or highways to its own manufacturing plant for use therein exclusively." The court held that there was no doubt that the public service commission had jurisdiction of the subject matter under section 74 of the public service commissions law, and added:

Nor can it be doubted that the J. and J. Rogers Company, organized under the Manufacturing Corporations Act of 1848, . . . is doing electric lighting for hire in violation of law. Indeed, it is conceded that this corporation is not authorized by its charter to do public and commercial lighting, involving the use of the public highways; and both at common law and under the provisions of section 10 of the General Corporation Law (Consol. Laws, ch. 23) the exercise of such powers is forbidden.

[1] Public Service Commission, Second District *v.* J. and J. Rogers Company, 184 N. Y. App. Div. 705 (1918).

It was the view of the court that the company had an "electric plant" as defined by the public service commission law;[1] that it came within the definition of an "electrical corporation" as given in the same statute;[2] and that it came within the jurisdiction of the court, therefore, under the provisions of the law.

It will be observed that Mr. Justice Woodward did not say that incorporation under the general manufacturing corporations act did not give the J. and J. Rogers Company capacity to receive a special franchise from the municipal authorities to use the streets for commercial lighting. Instead he said that the company was "doing electric lighting for hire in violation of law," since its *charter* did not authorize the company to use the public highways in doing "public and commercial lighting," and since "both at common law and under the provisions of section 10 of the General Corporation Law . . . the exercise of such powers" was forbidden. The court expressly stated that the company came within the definition, as given in the public service commissions law, of an electrical corporation, and that the subject matter was within the jurisdiction of the commission.[3] The

1 Section 2, subdivision 12.

2 Section 2, subdivision 13.

3 Commissioner Kracke, in the memorandum upon granting the application of the Kings County Company to merge into itself the Edison Company (case no. 2351), states the definition of an electrical corporation and an electric plant as set forth in the public service commissions law (*Supra*, p. 119); and draws the following conclusions regarding the companies concerned, citing at the close of the conclusions the above case of the Public Service Commission, Second District *v.* J. and J. Rogers Company:

"Each of the companies is a corporation owning, operating or managing an electric plant and is not within the exceptions. The mere fact that either of them was organized under the Manufacturing Corporations Act of 1848 (Laws of 1848, Chapter 40 as amended) would not affect the applicability of the provisions of the Public Service Commission Law to it. (Public Service Commission, Second District *v.* J. and J. Rogers Co., 184 App. Div. 705)." *Memorandum*, p. 4.

company made no claim of having received a franchise from the town authorities, or of being other than a manufacturing corporation. It contended that it was not an electric corporation, admitted that it was organized under the manufacturing act, and held that it had an "implied franchise" from the town in which it was operating. The court clearly found against the claim of the company to a franchise by acquiescence. What the court would have said concerning the company's claim to an implied franchise had the charter of the company expressly authorized it to do "public and commercial lighting" by electricity, cannot be known. Nor is it clear what attitude would have been taken by the court had the argument of the company taken the form of contending that since it was incorporated under the manufacturing act, and since the generation of electric current constitutes manufacturing, it would have implied power to receive a franchise for commercial electric lighting. The interesting suggestions directly touching upon the manufacturing corporations act of 1848 appear in the allegations of the public service commission of the second district to the effect that the company was "disqualified to be permitted to transmit or distribute electricity as a public service corporation by the petitioner, not having been incorporated under the Transportation Corporations Law;" and in the statement made by the lower court, namely, "If it is a manufacturing corporation, it cannot do an electrical business." [1]

[1] On page 7 of the brief on behalf of the intervenor-respondent, the Northern Adirondack Power Company, the following significant expression was used: "The Rogers Company is a manufacturing corporation having no provision in its charter for an electric business *and organized under Chapter 40 of the Laws of 1848, which act did not authorize the incorporation of companies for the purpose of doing a public electric business.* (Italics not in brief). Even stronger is an earlier statement: "The law of its [the Rogers Company's] original incorporation (Chapter 40, Laws of 1848) and the acts amendatory thereof and supplemental thereto did not authorize corporations incor-

Whatever the significance of this case, it does not seem probable that apart from the franchises connected with Brooklyn companies incorporated under the manufacturing corporations act, the validity of franchises held by the present operating electric light companies of New York will be challenged because of the fact that these grants were obtained in certain instances by companies incorporated under this manufacturing act. It is reasonable to believe that chapter 73 of the laws of 1882 made clear the right of "any corporation duly organized under the laws of this state for manufacturing and using electricity for producing light, heat and power" to "use electricity as the means of lighting streets . . . and public and private dwellings of cities . . . within this state."[1]

porated thereunder to engage in such business [distributing and selling electric current for light, heat and power purposes]." The latter statement is from an "opinion" of the second deputy attorney-general on July 7, 1916, prefacing his recommendation that an application of the Northern Adirondack Power Company be granted. The petition prayed that the charter of the Rogers Company be vacated and the corporate existence of the company annulled. The recommendation of the second deputy attorney-general was approved by the attorney-general on July 14, 1916. The "opinion" is found on page 52 in the documents filed in the case on appeal in Public Service Commission, Second District, *v.* J. and J. Rogers Company.

[1] *Supra*, p. 109.

CHAPTER V

THE PROBLEMS OF ACQUIESCENCE AND PERPETUITY

THE various reasons for questioning the validity of many of the franchises held by the Richmond Light and Railroad Company, Electricity Division, were stated in the second chapter, special stress being placed upon the possible incapacity of the predecessor company as original grantee, the New York and Staten Island Electric Company, to receive many of them.[1] Further, the Report concluded that the New York and Queens Electric Light and Power Company held no franchise for the former villages of Jamaica and Richmond Hill, save the grant to erect poles on Broadway in the latter village.[2] In the case of the Westchester Lighting Company, with respect to the franchise originally granted on May 28, 1895, by the board of trustees of the village of Eastchester to the Eastchester Electric Company, there has been set forth the claim of the present operating company that even assuming the expiration of the franchise at the end of five years, a franchise has since been acquired by acquiescence.[3] If the acquiescence theory has arisen in regard to the three operating companies mentioned,[4] how far

[1] Maltbie, *Franchises of Electrical Corporations in Greater New York*, p. 204.

[2] *Ibid.*, pp. 137-141.

[3] *Ibid.*, p. 70.

[4] "This theory of franchise by acquiescence has been urged in the case of the Westchester Lighting Company, the New York and Queens Electric Light and Power Company and the Richmond Light and Railroad Company. . . " *Ibid.*, p. 10.

may it be pressed in the event of the interjection of new technicalities affecting the validity or duration or existence of franchises held by the other operating companies? The year 1918 witnessed a determined challenge of the franchises in the system of the Edison Electric Illuminating Company of Brooklyn; and the burden of defense of the system has fallen, in 1919, upon the Brooklyn Edison Company, Inc. What foundation has the claim of franchise by acquiescence?

Perhaps the most important case that could be cited in favor of the acquiescence doctrine was, until recent date, that of the Richmond Gas Company *v.* Cromwell,[1] in which a decision was rendered in the appellate division in 1903.

The Richmond County Gas Light Company was incorporated in 1856 under chapter 37 of the laws of 1848 for the purpose of supplying gas in the towns of Northfield, Castleton, and Southfield. These towns were later incorporated into the city of New York. Through consolidation the rights of the company passed to the New York and Richmond Gas Company. After the commissioner of water supply, gas, and electricity of the city of New York had refused an application of the company presented March 9, 1903, for a permit to lay mains in some of the streets of the original towns which had not yet been occupied, and had based his refusal upon the grounds that the company had failed to show that it had secured the consent of the municipal authorities of the original towns of Castleton, Northfield and Southfield, the company moved for an alternative writ of mandamus. The supreme court, at special term in the county of Kings, through an order entered on May 5, 1903, denied the motion. The company appealed. The case was brought before the appellate division of the supreme

[1] New York and Richmond Gas Company *v.* Cromwell, 89 N. Y. App. Div. 291 (1903).

court of the second department, where a decision was given in December of the same year. The court held that the order appealed from should be reversed and the application for an alternative writ of mandamus granted. The court in its opinion pointed out that the broad and general grant of power in the statute under which the Richmond County Company had been organized was conditioned upon the consent of the municipal authorities and the reasonable regulations they might prescribe. The court was very clear in its attitude toward the charge made by respondent concerning the alleged failure of the gas company to secure the consent of the municipal authorities of the original towns. In referring to chapter 37 of the laws of 1848 the court stated:

> No method of manifesting this consent is pointed out; no definite body or bodies in the cities, villages or towns are pointed out, and the fair and reasonable inference is that any body that represents the community in a general sense, or in respect to the public rights which are to be granted, is authorized to give this consent. . . . It is sufficient, for the purposes of this case, to hold that the action of the highway commissioners of these several towns in the year 1856, acquiesced in without objection for nearly half a century, in the absence of a plain provision to the contrary, raises a presumption of the consent of all of the municipal authorities of the several towns. . . . This result would, it seems to us, under the authorities cited, follow even were it not possible to show any formal action on the part of the highway commissioners, for it is not suggested that the corporation did not construct its plant and distribute its gas in these several towns nearly half a century ago. . . . To say at this late day that the respondents may deny to the relator its rights under its franchise, upon any technical question growing out of the manner of the consent given so long ago, is to give precedence to unimportant forms above the substantial requirements of justice.

Another important case concerning the doctrine of acquiescence is that of the Flatbush Gas Company *v.* Coler. The supreme court supported the doctrine; [1] the appellate division affirmed the decision of the lower court; [2] but the court of appeals reversed the decision of the appellate division.[3]

The Flatbush Gas Company distributed electricity throughout the town of Flatbush before that municipality was incorporated into the city of Brooklyn. It held a valid franchise granting that right. After the town was annexed to the city of Brooklyn, the company entered into a contract with the commissioner of parks of Brooklyn to supply electric lights along Ocean Parkway, an avenue outside of the territory included in the former town of Flatbush. On August 4, 1897, the park commissioner made another contract with the company. The terms of this later agreement required the company to remove the poles erected under the earlier contract, and to supply electricity along Ocean Parkway by means of underground conduits. The terms also stated that the company might use the conduits laid in the parkway to supply electricity to private as well as to public consumers. In 1907 the company applied to the president of the borough of Brooklyn for a permit to open Ocean Parkway, in the thirty-first ward of the borough of Brooklyn, at the corner of Avenue I, for the purpose of connecting buildings on abutting lands with electrical wires maintained by the company in the parkway. The permit was refused on the ground that the company had never received from the proper authorities [4] a franchise to use the parkway

[1] Flatbush Gas Company *v.* Coler, 54 N. Y. Misc. 21 (1907).

[2] Flatbush Gas Company *v.* Coler, 121 N. Y. App. Div. 898 (1907).

[3] Flatbush Gas Company *v.* Coler, 190 N. Y. 268 (1907).

[4] The proper authorities were held by the city to be respectively the common council of the former city of Brooklyn, the board of aldermen of the city of New York, or the present franchise-granting authority of the city, the board of estimate and apportionment.

for supplying private consumers. The company moved for a peremptory writ of mandamus to direct the issuance of the permit, contending that under the contract of August 4, 1897, it held the right to use the parkway for the purpose of furnishing electricity to private as well as to public consumers. Judge Crane, in the special term of April, 1907, granted the writ. In rendering the opinion of the court, he cited the case of the Richmond Gas Company *v.* Cromwell, and said in part:

> But if it be that the provisions of the charter above quoted from mean, as the corporation counsel claims, that the park department had full and exclusive control of the Ocean parkway, subject to the powers of the common council as in the case of Prospect Park, then, as the Flatbush Gas Company entered upon the highway, under the contract of 1898, laid its wires, and has furnished light to the city and others for the past ten years, it must be presumed that the common council of the city of Brooklyn and the other municipal authorities succeeding that body have consented to such user, construction and operation. Richmond Gas Company *v.* Cromwell, 89 App. Div. 291.

The appellate division affirmed without opinion the order of the lower court. The court of appeals, however, held that while the park authorities concededly had the power to confer the right to use the parkway for lighting purposes necessary to the public enjoyment of the parkway itself, they did not have the jurisdiction to allow the use of that parkway for appliances for supplying electricity to private consumers. The court concluded, therefore, that since the company had not obtained local consent for private lighting from the proper franchise-granting authority, the order for a peremptory writ of mandamus should be reversed and its application denied.

In 1913 the board of estimate and apportionment of the

city of New York brought about a change in the plan and construction of the roadway and sidewalks of Eighth Avenue. In 1915 the city of New York, by virtue of the power vested in it to protect those using the highways, demanded through its board of aldermen that the New York Railways Company re-locate a certain street-railway track. The track in question had been constructed by a lessor company, incorporated in 1855 under the general railroad law.[1] On November 12, 1915, the appellate division of the supreme court in the first department [2] affirmed an order of special term which denied a motion for an alternative writ of mandamus to compel the company to comply with the demand for re-location of the track in question. The city carried the case to the court of appeals, where it was argued on January 6, 1916, and decided on February 29, 1916.[3] The court of appeals held that the appellant's direction to re-locate the tracks was *ultra vires*, and found that the order of the appellate division should be affirmed. In commenting upon the subdivision of the general railroad law which provided that nothing in the law should be construed to authorize the construction of any railroad, not already located in the city, without the consent of the corporation of such city, the opinion contained the following significant expressions:

> The record does not disclose to us the form or substance of the consent. When a railroad has been constructed and operated for a long period of time the courts will presume that an assent required by law was given. We must conclusively presume, in the absence of allegation and proof, that the tracks

[1] *Laws of New York*, 1850, ch. 140.

[2] People *ex rel.* City of New York *v.* New York Railways Company, 171 N. Y. App. Div. 910 (1915).

[3] People *ex rel.* City of New York *v.* New York Railways Company, 217 N. Y. 310 (1916).

of the company were lawfully placed and have lawfully remained in their present location. . . . The assent did not reserve to the city the power to withdraw it or cancel it or impose as a condition the right of the city to direct a relocation of the tracks. . . . It having been given, the purpose of the statute was fulfilled.

This case is an exceedingly important one. In the first place, the decision of the court of appeals is nine years later than that of the same court in the Flatbush Gas Company case. Moreover, in the New York Railways Company case, the court gave considerable support to the acquiescence doctrine, stressing the point that the court presumed conclusively, "in the absence of allegation and proof, that the tracks of the company were lawfully placed and have lawfully remained in their present location"; and, again, "When a railroad has been constructed and operated for a long period of time, the courts will presume that an assent required by law was given." It is true that the court of appeals in the Flatbush Gas Company case did not support in any way the idea of franchise by acquiescence; on the contrary, its decision compelled the Flatbush Gas Company to seek a franchise from the proper authorities of the city of New York for the desired operations on Ocean Parkway. The court simply did not discuss the acquiescence theory at all. No reference was made to the important Richmond Gas Company case, which was cited by Judge Crane in the supreme court to justify the granting of a peremptory writ of mandamus to the company.

In spite of its leaning toward the doctrine, it can scarcely be said that the New York Railways Company case supports the doctrine of acquiescence without qualification. The court employs the guarded phrase, "in the absence of allegation and proof." Had the city alleged and proved that no consent or improper consent had been given the company, the decision might have been in accord with the Flatbush case.

The *New York Law Journal* of December 13, 1917, reports Mr. Justice Delehanty's decision at the New York special term in the actions instituted by the city of New York against the Central Union Gas Company, the Northern Union Gas Company and the Westchester Lighting Company [1] on the alleged grounds that the companies possessed no special franchises to occupy certain streets in the city. It was held that the complaint should be dismissed upon the merits in each case. In the opinion of the court, the companies had proved their possession of franchises originally granted to their predecessors by local authorities of the political subdivisions later incorporated into the city of New York and embracing the disputed territory; and the municipality, by accepting the special franchise taxes regularly paid by the companies, was estopped from claiming that the companies did not possess valid franchises. The court stressed the point that the statutory requirement that the consent of the local authorities to the exercise of a special franchise be obtained had been met by the companies; and made it clear that long acquiescence by the municipal authorities in the occupation of the streets by the companies constituted such consent. The opinion on that point reads:

The plaintiff contends that these defendants have never obtained such consent. No particular method of giving the consent in question has ever been prescribed by the Legislature of this state, and it has been frequently decided that any conduct on the part of a municipality which is equivalent to acqui-

[1] City of New York *v.* Central Union Gas Company; Same *v.* Northern Union Gas Company; Same *v.* Westchester Lighting Company. *The New York Law Journal*, December 13, 1917.

escence in the use of the streets by a corporation having the legislative authority to occupy the same will be held to constitute the statutory consent. . . . In the cases at bar, the right and duty of each company to supply gas to the city and its inhabitants have been recognized and enforced by the city in innumerable contracts, resolutions and orders, upon which the companies have acted, and in reliance upon these established relations between the companies and the city the companies have laid many miles of mains and expended large amounts of capital in the development and maintenance of their respective businesses. . . . Such affirmative conduct of the municipality in directing a company to perform acts which necessitate the exercise of its franchise and the expenditure of capital will effectually stop the municipality from subsequently asserting that it never gave its consent to the use of the streets.

The Holmes Electric Protective Company was incorporated on January 29, 1883, under the telegraph act.[1] The articles of incorporation stated that the purposes of organization were to carry on a general telegraph and electric protection business and to construct and operate telegraph lines both within and without the limits of the state of New York. The company never carried on a general telegraph business of receiving and transmitting messages. From the time of its incorporation it obtained permits from different departments of the city regarding street work necessary to carry on its business, and it occupied the streets both with overhead wires and underground electrical conductors in the pursuit of its business of protecting premises against burglary and fire. Eventually, the city raised objections to the company's using the streets without having a special franchise. The company brought suit on the ground that it had a valid franchise from the time of its incorporation in 1883 to construct and maintain electrical conductors in the

[1] *Laws of New York*, 1848, ch. 265.

streets of the city, and asked that the city be enjoined from interfering with it and from demanding any sum to be paid as purchase price of a special franchise. The company maintained that even if it could be shown that it had not obtained from the state the right to use the streets of the city of New York without a preliminary consent from the municipal authorities, yet a valid franchise had been established by acquiescence. In October, 1916, the trial court held that the company was unauthorized in assuming that it had the corporate powers and franchise of a telegraph company so far as its real business was concerned, and also found against the company in respect to the claim of franchise by acquiescence. The complaint of the company was accordingly dismissed.[1] The plaintiff appealed. On January 18, 1918, the decision of the court in the appellate division, first department,[2] affirmed the judgment of the lower court upon the ground that the plaintiff had not procured the necessary preliminary consent of the municipal authorities to construct, maintain, and operate electrical conductors in the streets of the city of New York.

The case of Public Service Commission, Second District, *v.* J. and J. Rogers Company is another late decision which tends toward putting a quietus upon the doctrine of franchises by acquiescence. That case, which was not carried beyond the appellate division, has already been discussed.[3]

A decision of the Supreme Court of the United States which is of interest because it lends some support to the acquiescence theory was rendered June 16, 1913, in the case

[1] Holmes Electric Protective Company *v.* Armstrong, 97 N. Y. Misc. 184 (1916).

[2] Holmes Electric Protective Company *v.* Williams, 181 N. Y. App. Div. 687 (1918).

[3] Public Service Commission, Second District *v.* J. and J. Rogers Company, 184 N. Y. App. Div. 705 (1918); *supra*, p. 140.

of the Old Colony Trust Company *v.* City of Omaha.[1] By an ordinance of December, 1884, the council of the city of Omaha granted "The New Omaha-Thompson-Houston Electric Light Company or assigns" the right to erect and maintain poles and wires in the streets of the city for the purpose of transacting a general electric light business. One of the provisions of the ordinance declared:

That whenever the city council shall by ordinance declare the necessity of removing from the public streets or alleys of the city of Omaha the telegraph, telephone or electric poles, or wires thereon constructed or existing, said company shall, within sixty days from the passage of such ordinance, remove all poles and wires from said streets and alleys by it constructed, used, and operated.

On May 26, 1908, the city council passed a resolution purporting to terminate the company's use of the streets in its pursuit of the business of distributing electricity for heat and power, and directly ordering the city electrician to disconnect all wires leading from the conduits and poles of the company for transmission of electricity to private persons and premises for heat and power purposes. The Old Colony Trust Company, the trustee in a mortgage executed by the company upon its property, including the grant under the ordinance of 1884, and, as such, representative of the bondholders, brought suit to enjoin the enforcement of the resolution. The district court of the United States for the district of Nebraska sustained the action of the city; but the Supreme Court of the United States reversed the decree. The court, in discussing the meaning of the phrase as used in the ordinance of 1884, "general electric light business," insisted that the phrase had been interpreted in actual practice by the company and the city up to the resolution of 1908

[1] Old Colony Trust Company *v.* City of Omaha, 230 U. S. 100 (1913).

as including distribution of electricity for heat and power, no less than for lighting. The city had acquiesced in such an interpretation of the phrase by collection of taxes imposed on receipts from heat and power operations and by purchase of current for power. Among other things, the court said:

In these and various other ways disclosed by the record the city acquiesced in, encouraged and directly sanctioned the action of the two companies in successively equipping and adjusting the electric plant, at great expense, for the distribution of electric current for power and heat, knowing that they were engaged therein under a claim of right under the ordinance of 1884.

The court cited many decisions of the highest court of the state of Nebraska to show that a uniform view had been taken in the construction of the constitution and statutes of the state, and maintained that they had the effect of showing that the grant made by the ordinance of 1884 was perpetual. The court considered that the decisions of the supreme court of Nebraska, in the construction of its own laws, was binding on the Supreme Court of the United States if not infringing upon rights secured by the constitution of the United States. The court quoted with approval the decision given by the supreme court of Nebraska in a case directly in point, the case of Omaha and Council Bluffs Street Railway Company *v.* City of Omaha,[1] in which the court said in part:

The company supposed that it had the power under its charter to engage in the business of which the defendants now complain, and the city by its officers and agents assumed that it had such power, and by its acts not only permitted, but in-

[1] Omaha and Council Bluffs Street and Railway Company *v.* City of Omaha, 90 Nebraska 6 (1911).

duced, the plaintiff to expend large sums of money, acquire valuable property, and enter into contract relations with the interveners and others to carry on that business. It follows that it would now be unjust and inequitable to permit the city to destroy plaintiff's property and business, which it has thus fostered and encouraged, without compensation, and also deprive the interveners of their contractual rights therein.

While in this case the Supreme Court deferred to the opinions of the Nebraska court in cases involving similar questions of law, this was done merely for the purpose of showing what the law of the state was at the time when the franchise contract was entered into. The question involved was a federal question—Did the ordinance of 1908 impair the obligation of the contract which obligation was to be found in the state law as interpreted by the state courts? The Supreme Court held that it did. The court further held, however, that the acquiescence in question did not give the company the right to extend its operations to other streets against the will of the city.

In the case of Town of Essex *v.* New England Telegraph Company of Massachusetts, argued before the Supreme Court of the United States November 5, 1915, and decided December 6, 1915,[1] there is some additional support for the doctrine of acquiescence. The New England Telegraph Company of Massachusetts, incorporated in 1884 as a telegraph company under the laws of that state, filed immediately after its incorporation a written acceptance of the obligations set forth in the congressional post-road act of 1866. The post-road act of 1866 declared in substance that all who submitted to the conditions imposed by the act were, as far as state interference was concerned, free to erect telegraph lines along any of the military or post roads of the

[1] Town of Essex *v.* New England Telegraph Company of Massachusetts, 239 U. S. 313 (1915).

United States. One of the statutes of Massachusetts gave selectmen of towns authority to grant citizens the power to establish and maintain in the town apparatus for telegraphic communication; but provided that enjoyment of such grant of right of way for any length of time should not give a legal right to the continued enjoyment of such easement.

In 1884 the company made application to the selectmen of Essex for a right of way, but there was no evidence that the application was granted. Immediately thereafter, however, the company erected lines, without opposition, along four miles of the town's highways. Evidence showed that no action was taken to interfere with the erection or maintenance of the lines; not only was their operation acquiesced in, but the re-location of half the poles in 1895 was carried on under the direction of a selectman. In 1905 the officers of the town refused the company's petition for location of poles, the need of repairs having made the location imperative; and they further asserted that they would prevent repairs and stop the operation of the lines within the limits of Essex. Thereupon, the telegraph company sought an injunction against the threatened interference and obtained a temporary injunction from the district court on September 5, 1905. The cause came on for final hearing in 1913, and the United States district court awarded a perpetual injunction which restrained the town from interfering with the company's line of telegraph or with its needs of location, relocation, resetting, repairs or changes. The court held that the post act of 1866 protected the company from such interference. Contending that the court had erroneously construed the act of 1866, the town of Essex carried the case to the Supreme Court of the United States. The ruling of the lower court was affirmed by the United States Supreme Court, with the modification that the injunction was not to restrain the selectmen from imposing reasonable regulations concerning the location and operation of the company's lines. The court said in part:

With full knowledge of all the circumstances, the town authorities permitted the location and construction of lines along the highways, and for more than twenty years acquiesced in their maintenance and operation. The company has expended large sums of money and perfected a great instrumentality of interstate and foreign commerce, in the continued operation of which both the general public and the Government have an important interest. . . . . In the circumstances, appellee has acquired the same Federal right to maintain and operate its poles and wires along the ways in question that would have attached had the selectmen granted a formal antecedent permit.

If the city of New York acquires the power to take over the business of furnishing electric light to public and private consumers, it must reckon with the fact that the electric light companies cannot be deprived of their special franchises except under the power of eminent domain and upon payment of their full value. The value of the special franchises would, naturally, be very much greater if they were in perpetuity than if they were limited to a definite term of years or if they constituted mere licenses or tenancies terminable upon notice. It may certainly be contended that unless a time duration is expressly stipulated in the consent or grant to occupy the streets, the special franchises are perpetual. By consulting the tables in the second chapter, which give a condensed analysis of the electric lighting franchises now applicable to the boroughs of the city of New York, it will be observed that the Manhattan and Brooklyn franchises are all without time limit; [1] three of the franchises of The Bronx contain stipulations as to dura-

[1] The franchise secured by the Flatbush Gas Company on December 28, 1909 is subject to the time limits imposed by the charter of Greater New York.

tion; three of the twenty-one Queens franchises are not unlimited as to time; two of the Richmond franchises are specifically limited; five have no time limit expressed; one contains the ambiguous statement that the grant is not revocable except by due process of law; and one is frankly perpetual. The report made by Mr. Maltbie to the public service commission for the first district calls attention to the decision in the case of Blaschko *v.* Wurster,[1] which, in its application to franchises granted after a certain date, interprets the phraseology of the charter of Greater New York as militating against the perpetual feature of such a franchise as the last-named Richmond grant.

A few cases from the highest courts of the states may be cited in reference to the doctrine of perpetuity resulting from the omission of a time limit. In New York the case of People *v.* O'Brien [2] is in point.

The Broadway Surface Railroad Company was incorporated on May 13, 1884. The common council of the city of New York passed a resolution on December 5, 1884, granting the company the right to construct and operate a street railroad in Broadway. No time limit was expressed. The company was dissolved by the legislature on May 4, 1886. The court of appeals held that the street rights or franchise survived the dissolution of the company, and that the title became vested in the trustees of the company as trustees for its creditors and stockholders. Commenting upon the legislature's lack of power to deprive the company of the franchise, the court said in part:

> It is, however, earnestly contended for the state that such a franchise is a mere license or privilege enjoyable during the life of the grantee only, and revocable at the will of the state.

[1] Blaschko *v.* Wurster, 156 N. Y. 437 (1898).

[2] People *v.* O'Brien, 111 N. Y. 1 (1888).

We believe this proposition to be not only repugnant to justice and reason, but contrary to the uniform course of authority in this country. . . . We are, therefore, of the opinion that the Broadway Surface Railroad Company took an estate in perpetuity in Broadway through its grant from the city, under the authority of the Constitution and the act of the legislature. . . . We are, therefore, of the opinion that the Broadway Surface Company took an indefeasible title to the land necessary to enable it to construct and maintain a street railroad in Broadway, and to run cars thereon for the transportation of freight and passengers, which survived its dissolution.

In opposition to the doctrine of perpetuity resulting from the omission of a time limit, is the recent Illinois case of People *v.* Commercial Telephone and Telegraph Company.[1] On March 7, 1910, the Westfall Telephone Company received, by means of an ordinance passed by the village of Crossville, Illinois, the grant of the right to erect and maintain in the streets of the village the appliances necessary for carrying on the work of a telephone system. On July 25, 1913, the company sold its tangible property and franchise rights to the Commercial Telephone and Telegraph Company. On January 20, 1914, the village authorities repealed, by ordinance, the franchise of 1910 granted to the Westfall Telephone Company on the ground that it had been forfeited by misuser. Notice was served upon the Commercial Telephone and Telegraph Company to remove its poles and lines from the streets. The company did not comply with the direction. Thereupon the city obtained from the circuit court of White county a judgment of ouster. The judgment was reviewed by the supreme court of the state of Illinois and affirmed. The court was clear in the stand taken against the idea that if no time limit is

[1] People *v.* Commercial Telephone and Telegraph Company, 277 Ill. 265 (1917).

expressed, the grant is to be considered as being perpetual: " The grant in the ordinance to the Westfall Telephone Company was not for a definite time, and was therefore limited to the life of that corporation." [1]

The case of Blair *v.* Chicago [2] is not precisely in point, although the general doctrine has a bearing. In this case the Supreme Court of the United States emphasizes the well-known rule that any ambiguity in the terms of the grant must be resolved in favor of the public.

In 1858 the common council of the city of Chicago passed an ordinance granting a group of persons the right to construct and operate certain horse railways in the streets of the city for twenty-five years from the date of the ordinance. In 1859 the legislature enacted that the persons mentioned in the above ordinance be constituted a body corporate under the name of the Chicago City Railway Company, with a corporate life of twenty-five years. The seventh section of the act expressly confirmed the ordinance of 1858. The tenth section constituted another group of persons a corporate body by the name of the North Chicago City Railroad Company, with corporate powers and obligations similar to those of the first company. The act specified that conditions of construction and operation be imposed by the city council of Chicago. Three months later the common council passed two ordinances giving consent to the two corporations to construct and operate railways along designated streets, the first company's franchise term being specified as that prescribed by the act of 1859, and

[1] The court was of the opinion that since the statutes of the state of Illinois did not expressly authorize the transfer of franchise rights, where, as in the case of the original grant to the Westfall Telephone Company, no reference was made to successors or assigns, the grant of 1910 was not assignable.

[2] Blair *v.* Chicago, 201 U. S. 400 (1906).

the other " for the full term of twenty-five years from the passage of this ordinance and no longer."

A statute of 1861 incorporated the Chicago West Division Railway Company for a term of twenty-five years, and authorized the company to acquire the rights and franchises of the Chicago City Railway Company. Agreements between the two corporations provided for the transfer of franchises over certain streets. In 1865 the legislature passed an act extending the corporate life of these two companies from twenty-five years to ninety-nine years each.[1]

It would scarcely be profitable to review the complicated facts necessary to an understanding of all the issues of the litigation that arose after the passage of the act of 1865. Controversy centered about the construction of an ambiguous phrase in the second section of the act, " during the life hereof." The companies construed the phrase as extending the term of their franchises to ninety-nine years from the date of the statutory enactment of 1865. The court held that only " the acts or deeds of transfer between the corporations so far as they relate to franchises which are not subject to the express limitations of the act " could be " consistently extended " for ninety-nine years.

The court was emphatic in stressing the rule that any ambiguity in the terms of the grant must be resolved in favor of the public:

> One who asserts private rights in public property under grants of the character of those under consideration, must, if he would establish them, come prepared to show that they have been conferred in plain terms, for nothing passes by the grant except it be clearly stated or necessarily implied. . . . It is matter of common knowledge that grants of this character

[1] The act was construed as having the effect of extending to a term of ninety-nine years the corporate life of the North Chicago City Railway Company as well.

are usually prepared by those interested in them, and submitted to the legislature with a view to obtain from such bodies the most liberal grant of privileges which they are willing to give. . . . "The just presumption in every such case is that the State has granted in express terms all that it designed to grant at all." [1]

The case of Boise Water Company *v.* Boise City [2] is directly in point upon the question of the duration of a franchise in which no time limit is expressed. In 1889 the city of Boise, Idaho, passed an ordinance granting to the Eastman brothers the right to lay and maintain water pipes in the streets of the city. The grantees constructed their plant and began operation. Similar rights were granted the next year to another company, and another water supply system was constructed. Shortly thereafter the Eastman brothers and the later grantee conveyed all their franchises and rights to the Boise Artesian Hot and Cold Water Company, Limited. In 1906 the city, maintaining that the ordinance of 1889 granted a mere license for an indefinite period, passed an ordinance requiring the company to pay a sum of three hundred dollars each month for the use of the streets of the city for laying and maintaining its pipes in the distributing system. The company claimed that the ordinance of 1906 was an impairment of the property right acquired by the company through the earlier ordinances and was in contravention of the contract clause of the constitution of the United States. The district court of the United States for the district of Idaho ruled that the ordinance of 1889 was a revocable license, and that the ordinance of 1906 was valid. The Supreme Court of the United States reversed the judgment. The court said:

[1] The quotation is from Cooley's *Constitutional Limitations*, p. 565.

[2] Boise Water Company *v.* Boise City, 230 U. S. 84 (1913).

The grant was made in contemplation of the investment of large capital in the construction of a system of water works for the permanent supply of the city with water. The presumption is that no such enterprise would have been entered upon if the street easement was subject to immediate revocation.

The case of Owensboro *v.* Cumberland Telephone and Telegraph Company [1] is another case in point. By an ordinance of December, 1889, the city of Owensboro, Kentucky, conferred upon the Cumberland Telephone and Telegraph Company, its successors and assigns, the right to erect and maintain a telephone system in the city. The grant was not exclusive, but no time limit was expressed. In January, 1909, the city council passed an ordinance requiring the telephone company to remove its poles and wires, and directing the mayor to have them removed in case the company failed to comply within a reasonable length of time. The company was given an alternative choice of purchasing a franchise to maintain the poles and wires and operate the system, under conditions to be prescribed by another ordinance to be passed when the company should make the request for passage. The company prayed for an injunction to restrain the enforcement of the ordinance on the ground that its contractual property rights in the streets were being impaired. The circuit court of the United States for the western district of Kentucky granted a permanent injunction against the enforcement of the ordinance. The city carried an appeal to the Supreme Court of the United States. There the decree of the court below was affirmed. In commenting upon the perpetuity feature of the municipal ordinance, Mr. Justice Lurton said:

[1] Owensboro *v.* Cumberland Telephone and Telegraph Company, 230 U. S. 58 (1913).

The grant by ordinance to an incorporated telephone company, its successors and assigns, of the right to occupy the streets and alleys of a city with its poles and wires for the necessary conduct of a public telephone business, is a grant of a property right in perpetuity, unless limited in duration by the grant itself or as a consequence of some limitation imposed by the general law of the state, or by the corporate powers of the city making the grant. . . . If there be authority to make the grant and it contains no limitation or qualification as to duration, the plainest principles of justice and right demand that it shall not be cut down, in the absence of some controlling principle of public policy. This conclusion finds support from a consideration of the public and permanent character of the business such companies conduct and the large investment which is generally contemplated. If the grant be accepted and the contemplated expenditure made, the right cannot be destroyed by legislative enactment or city ordinance based upon legislative power, without violating the prohibitions placed in the Constitution for the protection of property rights. To quote from a most weighty writer upon municipal corporations,[1] in approving of the decision in People *v.* O'Brien:[2] . . . . "The grant to the Railway Company may or may not have been improvident on the part of the municipality, but having been made and the rights of innocent investors and of

[1] Dillon, *Municipal Corporations*, fifth edition, section 1265.

[2] People *v.* O'Brien, 111 N. Y. 1, 42 (1888).

In the case of Detroit United Railway Company *v.* Detroit 229 U. S. 39, the Supreme Court of the United States refused, in 1913, to hold that the effect of a certain ordinance of 1906 was to extend to 1921 the period of franchises, with original terms ending in 1910. The court stressed the opinion that franchises granting rights of the public must be strictly construed against the grantee. The court cited the case of Blair *v.* Chicago, 201 U. S. 400, 471, and the case of Cleveland Electric Railway Company *v.* Cleveland, 204 U. S. 116, 129, in support of the rule of strict construction. In the latter case Mr. Justice Peckham said: "The rules of construction which have been adopted by courts in cases of public grants of this nature by the authorities of cities are of long standing."

third parties as creditors and otherwise having intervened, it would have been a denial of justice to have refused to give effect to the franchise according to its tenor and import, when fairly construed. . . . In the absence of language expressly limiting the estate or right of the company, we think the court correctly held under the legislation and facts that the right created by the grant of the franchise was perpetual and not for a limited term only."

From this decision four justices dissented.[1]

One of the important recent decisions involving the question of perpetuity of franchises is that rendered on January 28, 1918, by the Supreme Court of the United States in the case of Northern Ohio Traction and Light Company *v.* State of Ohio.[2] On February 22, 1892, the board of county commissioners of Stark County, Ohio, passed a resolution granting to William Lynch and such railroad corporation as he might cause to be incorporated for that purpose the right to construct and operate an electric railroad along certain definite sections of the state highway. No time limit was expressed in the contract. By successive assignments, the rights under the contract passed to the company named. On February 19, 1913, following a disagreement with the company concerning rates, the county commissioners adopted a resolution declaring that the term of the grant of 1892 was terminated by the later resolution of 1913, and that such termination was justified by the fact that the term of the grant of 1892 was an indeterminate one, continuing from day to day, subject to termination at any time by either party to the grant. The resolution directed the prosecuting attorney of Stark County, Ohio, to take the legal proceedings necessary to have the grant of

[1] Justices Day, McKenna, Hughes, and Pitney.

[2] Northern Ohio Traction and Light Company *v.* State of Ohio, 245 U. S. 574 (1918).

1892 made null and void, and the electric railway itself removed. The prosecuting attorney accordingly instituted proceedings in the supreme court of Ohio. Without any written opinion, the supreme court of Ohio on October 19, 1915,[1] decreed that the defendant company be ousted from the exercise of the franchise described, and ordered it to remove the tracks and switches from the road in question. Contending that the commissioners' resolution of February 19, 1913, was an impairment of contract, a taking of property without due process of law, and a denial of the equal protection of the laws, the company carried the case to the Supreme Court of the United States. There the judgment of the supreme court of the state of Ohio was reversed, and the case remained for further proceedings. Mr. Justice Reynolds, who delivered the opinion of the court, said in part:

> The circumstances surrounding the grant of 1892 show no intention either to give or accept a mere revocable right. It would be against common experience to conclude that rational men wittingly invested large sums of money in building a railroad subject to destruction at any moment by mere resolution of the county commissioners. . . . . Where there are no controlling provisions in state constitutions or statutes and no prior adjudication by its courts to the contrary, we have distinctly held that franchises like the one under consideration are contracts not subject to annulment as here undertaken.

Closely following upon the decision in the Northern Ohio Traction case came the decision of the Supreme Court in the case of City of Covington *v.* South Covington and Cincinnati Street Railway Company.[2]

[1] State of Ohio *ex rel.* Pontius *v.* Northern Ohio Traction Light Company, 114 N. E. 53 (1915).

[2] City of Covington *v.* South Covington and Cincinnati Street Railway Company, 246 U. S. 413 (1918).

In December, 1864, the council of the city of Covington, Kentucky, passed an ordinance entitled, "An ordinance prescribing the terms and conditions of street passenger railroads within the city of Covington." The ordinance provided for receiving bids to construct such railroads and declared that any contract made under its provisions was to be limited to a term of twenty-five years. In conformity with the terms of this general ordinance, the Covington Street Railway Company obtained from the city the right to operate a street railway on designated streets. In December, 1869, there was passed another ordinance, stating that " all the authority and right that the city of Covington has the capacity to, be and the same hereby is granted to E. F. Abbott . . . . to construct, hold and operate a street railroad " upon the streets named. Abbott and his associates were incorporated, following the passage of the ordinance, as the Covington and Cincinnati Street Railway Company, with perpetual succession, and general authority to construct railways in the city of Covington along streets designated by the council. No provision was made in the ordinance of December, 1869, for the termination of the grant, outside of forfeiture in the event that the grantees failed to keep their covenants. On December 20, 1876, the Covington and Cincinnati Street Railway Company turned over its right under contracts and ordinances to the South Covington and Cincinnati Street Railway Company. The latter company was incorporated in January, 1876, with practically the same powers as the former. An ordinance of 1881 recognized that all the rights acquired by Abbott had been conveyed to the South Covington and Cincinnati Street Railway Company. In 1882 the South Covington and Cincinnati Street Railway Company purchased the lines of the rival company, the Covington Street Railway. According to the twenty-five-year limitation in the ordinance of 1864, the franchise of the latter company had but eight years left to run.[1]

The South Covington and Cincinnati Street Railway Company was authorized specifically to take over its rival's lines by an ordinance passed by the city council. The ordinance specified that the purchasing company, in its contemplated occupation of the streets in which the right of way was being held by the Covington Street Railway Company, would be "subject to the conditions, limitations, and restrictions contained in the ordinances regulating its [the South Covington and Cincinnati Street Railway's] right to the streets now occupied by the said South Covington and Cincinnati Street Railway Company."

On July 14, 1913, the city passed an ordinance providing for the award of a twenty-year franchise for a street railway to the best bidder. The South Covington and Cincinnati Street Railway Company brought a bill in equity to restrain the city from carrying out the ordinance. The company claimed by grant and contract the right over the same streets designated in the ordinance. It set up the contract clause and the fourteenth amendment of the federal constitution. The city maintained that the grant of the company had expired, and that it would not have been within the power of the city to confer the perpetual franchises claimed by the company. The district court granted the injunction and the city appealed. The Supreme Court of the United States upheld the decision of the lower court. In referring to the Abbott grant of 1869, Mr. Justice Holmes said:

As there is no hint at any limitation of time in the grant to Abbott, and, on the other hand, the city grants all the right and

[1] The ordinance provided that the company at the expiration of the original franchise period might make bids for a new franchise, and that it should be compensated for its property in case that another company became the successful bidder.

authority that it has the capacity to grant, there can be no question that the words taken by themselves purport a grant in perpetuity more strongly than those held to have that effect in Owensboro *v.* Cumberland Telephone and Telegraph Company (230 U. S. 58). . . . The question of the power of the city to grant a perpetual franchise needs but a few words. By statute the streets were "vested in the city" and the authorities of the city were given "exclusive control over the same," and in another section the council was given "exclusive power to establish and regulate . . . all sidewalks, streets, alleys, lanes, spaces and commons of the city." . . . No decision of the state court is brought to our attention that calls for any hesitation in following the authority of Owensboro *v.* Cumberland Telephone and Telegraph Company . . . and pronouncing the authority complete.

In both the Northern Ohio Traction and Light Company case and the South Covington and Cincinnati Street Railway Company case, Mr. Justice Clarke and Mr. Justice Brandeis dissented from the opinion of the majority of the court.[1] Mr. Justice Clarke, in his dissenting opinion in the latter case, feelingly observed:

[1] Both justices dissented also in the case of Owensboro *v.* Owensboro Water Works Company, 243 U. S. 166 (1917). Mr. Justice Clarke said: "This case presents for decision the single but very important question whether the City of Owensboro, Kentucky, by ordinance passed on June 3, 1889, granted to the Owensboro Water Works Company a franchise renewable indefinitely and therefore in effect perpetual or only a franchise for twenty-five years "to maintain, complete and operate" water works in that city. . . . It may be that the settled conviction which I have that no legislator, congressman, or councilman would knowingly consent to grant perpetual rights in public streets to a private corporation has so darkened my understanding that I cannot properly appreciate the point of view of my associates and the reasons advanced in support of it, but, however this may be, the reasons stated in this opinion convince me that the grant under discussion was not in effect a perpetual grant."

The decision in the case was to the effect that the life of the franchise granted by an ordinance of 1889 was not limited to twenty-five years,

Fully realizing the futility, for the present, of dissenting from what seems to me to be an unfortunate extension of the doctrine of the Owensboro case, 230 U. S. 58, I deem it my duty to record my dissent, with the hope for a return to the sound, but now seemingly neglected, doctrine of Blair *v.* Chicago, 201 U. S. 400, 463, declaring that a corporation which would successfully assert a private right in a public street must come prepared to show that it has been conferred "in plain terms," "in express terms," and that any ambiguity in the terms of the grant must be resolved in favor of the public and against the corporation, "which can claim nothing which is not clearly given." The reason given by the court for this rule is, that "grants of this character are usually prepared by those interested in them," and that "it serves to defeat any purpose concealed by the skillful use of terms, to accomplish something not apparent on the face of the act." This is declared to be "sound doctrine which should be vigilantly observed and enforced." . . . . Believing that the application of this wise rule to the decree before us must result in its reversal, I dissent from the opinion of the court.

From the cases discussed above it is manifest that the Supreme Court is thus far committed to the doctrine that a franchise in which no time limit is fixed is a grant in perpetuity. Such a grant is protected by the contract clause of the federal constitution unless it can be shown that under

and that the phrase in the ordinance which put the term of the grant "for and during the existence of the said corporation" was evidence confirming the court's opinion that the life of the franchise was meant to last as long as the corporate life of the Owensboro Water Works Company lasted by extension beyond the twenty-five-year period. The court made a special point with reference to the perpetuity of the grant:

"Of the suggestion that under this view the franchise may be made perpetual by repeated extensions of the plaintiff's corporate life, it is enough to say that we are here concerned with but a single extension already effected. The statute permitting such extensions may not be in force when the present twenty-five year period expires, and, if it be in force, nothing may be done under it."

the law of the state, at the time the grant was made, it could not have been given in perpetuity.

As far as the city of New York is concerned, the granting of perpetual franchises since 1897 has been expressly forbidden by the Greater New York charter. Section seventy-three provides:

> After the approval of this act no franchise or right to use the streets, avenues, waters, rivers, parkways, or highways of the city shall be granted by any board or officer of the City of New York under the authority of this act to any person or corporation for a longer period than twenty-five years, except as herein provided, but such grant may, at the option of the city, provide for giving to the grantee the right on a fair revaluation or revaluations to renewals not exceeding in the aggregate twenty-five years.

Few would dispute that the policy of granting perpetual franchises for public utilities would today meet with general disapproval. The city, however, is faced with the situation that the overwhelming majority of the grants held by the present operating electric light companies are franchises with no time limit expressed.

To many it appears an intolerable situation that perpetual rights in the streets should be possessed by private corporations. Persons holding this view are often not agreed among themselves as to the feasibility or desirability of municipal ownership of public utilities. They hold differing opinions, moreover, regarding the policy to be pursued by the city in the event that municipal ownership is introduced. Some hold that the city should own the utilities but should permit private operation; others consider that the city ought to operate its own utilities. Municipal ownership and operation for profit is a plan advocated on one hand; on the other, there is advanced the suggestion that the better plan would be to conduct the utilities for the general well-being of the people, and support the undertaking in whole or in part by taxes. But most people are agreed in the opinion that the city ought to have control of its own streets, at least to the extent that it should not be compelled to allow private corporations to occupy the streets in perpetuity and to derive returns upon the value of the intangible right.

The position is taken by many that the perpetual franchises held by public utility companies may be taxed, and the rates reduced until the valuation due to the intangible element of the franchise disappears. This position is frequently defended on legal and ethical grounds. Obviously, to increase taxation and decrease rates allowed for service is to take away property; but the process is legal up to the point where the courts decide that it has become confiscation. Broadly speaking, the ethical defense of the position lies in the extent to which it serves the public interest. The statement is advanced that the courts are too often conservative, and that the law lags behind the advanced public opinion which would break the companies' hold upon streets. Many, however, entertain the hopeful view that the judiciary are viewing technicalities, not as an end in themselves, but as factors to be considered in the light of social needs and claims.

Much importance is attached by many to the fact that the perpetual franchises of today were granted carelessly in the past by municipal authorities that had no conception of the enormous future value of the rights they heedlessly conferred. Moreover, there is pressed with confidence the claim that bribery and other forms of corruption were employed by the individuals or companies obtaining the grants. The history of corruption in public utilities makes lurid reading. Today the demand is heard that the mistakes of the past be rectified. It is not contended that no suffering will result from the elimination of values based upon present monopoly rights in the public streets. It is conceded that creditors and innocent investors will be involved to their detriment in the tangled mesh of franchise problems. But the gift of the city's streets, carelessly bestowed or corruptly obtained in the long ago, should not be held as a perpetual privilege and used to bolster the capitalization upon which a company is entitled to a return in higher rates or reduced service at the expense of the great body of citizens. "A fair profit" may be allowed to the company, certainly; but the fair profit should not include a return upon a valuation placed upon the intangible right to occupy the streets in perpetuity.[1] Such an adjustment of the situation would remove the very source of that power which makes public utilities often the center of political attention, and would ensure, more certainly, uncorrupted public service commissions if regulation under private ownership continues.

A diametrically opposed point of view is vigorously defended by those who believe that the companies are entitled to enjoy returns on the intangible as well as the tangible part of their special franchises, as long as they give adequate service at "reasonable rates." They who adopt this attitude believe that we must deplore the spirit of hostility which often obtains toward the companies in possession of perpetual franchise rights. They hold that people who approach the study of franchise problems with the preliminary conviction that public utility corporations are crafty enemies of a city's interests, are far too prone to place an antagonistic construction upon all those acts of omission and deeds of commission on the part of public service commis-

[1] The increasing number of public utilities which are going into the hands of receivers demonstrates that the idea of "fair profits" must be regarded as merely a general conception.

sions and courts which are not clearly conducive to reducing the strength of the companies. In such an environment of indiscriminate criticism, public service commissions find themselves assailed with charges of collusion with the company whenever they establish valuations for rate-making or purchase, or allow issues of bonds or changes in intercorporate relationships. In the same manner, unreasoning reproach is too often heaped upon the courts in any decision made in the company's favor. The judge runs a gamut of charges, ranging all the way from the statement that he has an unfair, reactionary, corporation or property bias to the sensational accusation that he keeps his position on the bench chiefly by subservience to the wishes of the company. Indeed, there is a danger that if those who are uncompromisingly hostile toward the companies have sufficiently ready access to the public ear, they may make it difficult for any but the most fearless public service commissioner and judge to deal impartially with the company. If a corporation opposes municipal ownership, it is stamped as a foe of legitimate civic aspirations; if it manifests willingness to witness the introduction of that policy, it is suspected of wanting to dump unprofitable utilities on the public. If it does not openly champion regulation by a public service commission, it is charged with indulging in the hope of aldermanic corruption; if it does accept cordially the commission plan of regulation and control because of what is a natural desire for systematic instead of sporadic regulation, it is proclaimed a power that has insidiously gained control of the commissions themselves. If it asks for a rate increase and substantiates the request by data evincing the need of such increase, it is viewed as one that seeks to prey upon a helpless people; if it goes into bankruptcy, it is adjudged a crafty, unscrupulous wrecker of the utility through nefarious manipulations.

They who, in defense of the companies, take this stand freely admit that the special privilege of occupying the streets lays upon the corporations the duty of paying taxes for the privilege and of furnishing adequate service at reasonable rates. They hold, moreover, that the inherently monopolistic character of the industry, coupled with the special use of the city streets, justifies extreme watchfulness on the part of the regulatory powers. But taxation should not be made a weapon of destruction unless warranted by social necessity; and there is no social necessity which calls for the use of the instrument of increased taxation together with decreased rates for service until capitulation to municipal ownership is the only alternative left to the companies.

They make no effort to deny that municipal corruption in public utilities was a real factor in the past. It is their contention that the companies were caught in the system of boss-rule and graft in general, and were, therefore, victims no less than authors of misrule. For the heedlessness and corruption of the past there is at least a two-sided responsibility. The city must be considered responsible for its share.

To some the argument is fallacious which asserts that the intangible right to occupy the streets was a gift to the companies for which no substantial return was made by the corporations, and for which, consequently, the city should not be expected to pay either in fares or as compensation in condemnation proceedings. Property is no less property for being a gift; and the right to occupy the streets is a property right in the fullest sense of the word. They maintain that it is not, however, correct to say that no payment was made even in the cases where the companies made no return in direct cash outlay. The returns that the electric-lighting companies gave by way of enormous impetus to the comforts and conveniences of civilization should be emphasized rather than minimized; and the initiative that moved to establish electric-lighting service in the political subdivisions that either could not or would not enter upon the undertaking themselves deserves commendation instead of condemnation.

BIBLIOGRAPHY

Bibliographical Note

It does not seem essential to give the long list of books and articles in which are discussed municipal ownership of public utilities and local and state regulation of municipal utilities. The principal secondary source in this study has been Milo R. Maltbie's *Franchises of Electrical Corporations in Greater New York*. Other helpful secondary sources were *Municipal Franchises* (two volumes), Delos F. Wilcox; *Report on the Tax Levies of the City of New York for the Years 1899 to 1914* inclusive, William A. Prendergast, Comptroller of the city of New York; *Report of the Mayor's Advisory Commission on Administration of the Tax Law, City of New York,* 1917; *Report of Commissioners of Taxes and Assessments of the City of New York*, 1918; and *Statistics of Light, Heat and Power Companies*, Volume III, a report of the public service commission for the first district of the state of New York for the year ending December 31, 1916. Valuable source material has been found in important briefs, in records in the bureau of real estate of corporations and special franchises in the department of taxes and assessments of New York City, in reports of the electric-lighting companies to the public service commission, and in the collection of documents in the filing department of the public service commission. *The New York Law Journal* has been consulted freely and the laws of the state of New York for 1848, 1879, 1882, 1890, 1892 and 1909 have been studied relative to the litigation involving franchise rights.

I. Cases

Blair *v.* Chicago, 201 U. S. 400.

Blaschko *v.* Wurster, 156 N. Y. 437.

Boise Water Company *v.* Boise City, 230 U. S. 84.

Brush Electric Manufacturing Company *v.* Wemple, 129 U. S. 543.

City of Covington *v.* South Covington and Cincinnati Street Railway Company, 246 U. S. 413.

City of New York *v.* Central Union Gas Company (Reported in *New York Law Journal,* December 13, 1917).

City of New York *v.* New York Railways Company, 171 N. Y. App. Div. 910.

City of New York *v.* New York Railways Company, 217 N. Y. 310.

Clements *v.* Edison Electric Illuminating Company of Brooklyn, 100 N. Y. Misc. 569 (1917).

Cleveland Electric Railway Company *v.* Cleveland, 204 U. S. 116.

Detroit United Railway Company *v.* Detroit, 229 U. S. 39.

Edison Electric Illuminating Company of New York *v.* Wemple, 129 N. Y. 665.

Edison Electric Illuminating Company of New York *v.* Wemple, 141 N. Y. 471.

Flatbush Gas Company *v.* Coler, 54 N. Y. Misc. 21.

Flatbush Gas Company *v.* Coler, 121 N. Y. App. Div. 898.

Flatbush Gas Company *v.* Coler, 190 N. Y. 268.

Holmes Electric Protective Company *v.* Armstrong, 97 N. Y. Misc. 184.

Holmes Electric Protective Company *v.* Williams, 181 N. Y. App. Div. 687.

Jamaica Water Supply Company *v.* Tax Commissioners, 128 N. Y. App. Div. 13.

Municipal Gas Company *v.* Rice, 138 N. Y. 151.

New York and Richmond Gas Company *v.* Cromwell, 89 N. Y. App. Div. 291.

Northern Ohio Traction and Light Company *v.* Ohio, 245 U. S. 574.

Old Colony Trust Company *v.* City of Omaha, 230 U. S. 100.

Omaha and Council Bluffs Street and Railway Company *v.* City of Omaha, 90 Nebraska, 6.

Owensboro *v.* Cumberland Telephone and Telegraph Company, 230 U. S. 58.

Owensboro *v.* Owensboro Water Works Company, 243 U. S. 166.

People *v.* Commercial Telephone and Telegraph Company, 277 Ill. 265.

People *v.* O'Brien, 111 N. Y. 1.

Public Service Commission, Second District, *v.* J. and J. Rogers Company, 103 N. Y. Misc. 711.

Public Service Commission, Second District, *v.* J. and J. Rogers Company, 184 App. Div. 705.

Smith *v.* Edison Electric Illuminating Company of Brooklyn, Williams, and Pounds.

Town of Essex *v.* New England Telegraph Company of Massachusetts, 239 U. S. 313.

Union Railway of New York City *v.* Tax Commissioners (Reported in *New York Law Journal*, April 17, 1913).

West Side Electric Company *v.* The Consolidated Telegraph and Electrical Subway Company, 187 N. Y. 58.

Willcox *v.* Consolidated Gas Company, 212 U. S. 19.

Wyandotte Electric Light Company *v.* City of Wyandotte, 124 Michigan, 43.

II. Documents in Filing Department of Commission

Copies of documents offered by Assistant Corporation Counsel in evidence at hearings concerning Cases Nos. 2351 and 2352 (Brooklyn Edison Company, Inc.—Applications for approval of merger, issuance of mortgage and issuance of bonds) and listed in the files of the Commission as follows:

I. Supreme Court, New York County, Amsterdam Electric Light, Heat and Power Company and Edison Electric Illuminating Company of Brooklyn, plaintiffs, *v.* William J. Gaynor as Mayor of the City of New York *et al.*, defendants (County Clerk No. 7950, Year 1911).

1. Printed copy of pleadings bound in a cover bearing the caption, Supreme Court, Appellate Division, First Department.
2. Statement of facts dated February 15, 1915, submitted by plaintiffs with a request that they be found by the Referee.
3. Statement of facts and requests to find dated March 15, 1915, submitted in behalf of defendants.
4. Opinion of Referee.
5. Memorandum by Referee.
6. Exceptions of plaintiff, Edison Electric Illuminating Company of Brooklyn, dated February 28, 1916.
7. Exceptions of plaintiff, Amsterdam Electric Light, Heat and Power Company, dated February 28, 1916.
8. Defendants' exceptions dated January 27, 1916.
9. Notice of motion by plaintiffs dated November 27, 1916, for an order remitting to Referee his report, etc., for purpose of an amended and corrected report.
10. Affidavit by Vincent Victory dated December 1, 1916, in opposition to motion to refer back report to Referee.
11. Memorandum opinion in *Law Journal*, December 15, 1916, by Mr. Justice Greenbaum, Supreme Court, Special Term, Part I, granting motion to remit to Referee.
12. Order dated December 22, 1916, by Mr. Justice Greenbaum, remitting report to Referee.
13. Notice of motion by plaintiffs dated January 15, 1917, for a resettlement of order of December 22, 1916.
14. Order by Mr. Justice Greenbaum dated January 31, 1917, resettling order of December 22, 1916.
15. Judgment of April 13, 1917, with notice of entry by plaintiffs.
16. Report of Referee dated March 19, 1917, with defendants' notice of filing dated April 23, 1917.
17. Report of Referee dated January 3, 1916, with defendants' notice of filing dated April 23, 1917.

18. Exceptions of plaintiff, Edison Electric Illuminating Company of Brooklyn, dated April 20, 1917, to the report of Referee.
19. Exceptions of Amsterdam Electric Light, Heat and Power Company dated April 20, 1917, to the report of Referee.
20. Exceptions dated April 23, 1917, by defendants.
21. Notice of Appeal by defendants dated May 1, 1917.
22. Notice of Appeal by Edison Electric Illuminating Company of Brooklyn dated May 10, 1917.

II. Supreme Court, County of Kings, Henry W. Smith against Edison Electric Illuminating Company of Brooklyn, William Williams as Commissioner of Water Supply, Gas and Electricity and Lewis H. Pounds as President of the Borough of Brooklyn.
1. Summons and complaint dated and verified July 13, 1917, Carr and Hill, plaintiff's attorneys, 120 Broadway.
2. Answer of defendants Williams and Pounds verified September 29, 1917.
3. Order dated August 9, 1917, made by Mr. Justice Scudder granting injunction.
4. Opinion by Mr. Justice Scudder, *New York Law Journal*, August 30, 1917, as to modification of injunction.

III. Supreme Court, Kings County, Re Application of Albert Clements for a peremptory writ of mandamus, etc., against Edison Electric Illuminating Company of Brooklyn and Amsterdam Electric Light, Heat and Power Company.
1. Alternative writ of mandamus allowed September 17, 1917, by Mr. Justice Benedict.

IV. Minutes of Board of Estimate and Apportionment, March 10, 1916, pages 1397 to 1400 inclusive.
1. Resolution directing Corporation Counsel to petition Attorney-General to institute action to forfeit franchise of Amsterdam Electric Light, Heat and Power Company on the ground of a non-user.
2. Resolution directing that in any permit issued by the President of the Borough of Brooklyn and the Commissioner of Water Supply, Gas and Electricity to the Edison Electric Illuminating Company of Brooklyn, in the thirtieth and thirty-second wards, a reservation be made as to the contest of the franchise rights of the company.
3. Resolution directing Corporation Counsel to advise Comptroller as to steps to be taken to safeguard interests of City in the event of the payment of any moneys in the future by the Amsterdam Company or the Edison Company.

III. Papers on Appeal

Papers on Appeal in the appellate division of the supreme court of the second department in the matter of the application of Albert Clements, *Respondent*, for a peremptory writ of mandamus directed to William Williams, as Commissioner of Water Supply, Gas and Electricity of the City of New York, and Lewis H. Pounds, as President of the Borough of Brooklyn, City of New York. Edison Electric Illuminating Company of Brooklyn, and Amsterdam Electric Light, Heat and Power Company, *Appellants*.

Notice of appeal.

Order appealed from.

Notice of motion for peremptory writ of mandamus.

Petition for peremptory writ of mandamus.

Exhibit "A"—annexed to petition (certificate of incorporation of the Edison Electric Illuminating Company of Brooklyn).

Exhibit "B"—(consent of common council to Edison Electric Illuminating Company of Brooklyn).

Exhibit "C"—(consents of common council of Brooklyn to Charles Cooper and Company and to Pope, Sewall and Company, granted May 19, 1884).

Exhibit "D"—(certificate of incorporation of the Municipal Electric Light Company).

Exhibit "E"—(certificate of incorporation of the Citizens Electric Illuminating Company of Brooklyn).

Exhibit "F"—(consent of common council to Kings County Electric Light and Power Company).

Exhibit "G"—(certificate of incorporation of Kings County Electric Light and Power Company).

Exhibit "H"—(certificate of incorporation of the State Electric Light and Power Company).

Exhibit "I"—(consent of the common council of Brooklyn granted to the State Electric Light and Power Company, December 30, 1895).

Exhibit "J"—(certificate of incorporation of Amsterdam Electric Light, Heat and Power Company).

Affidavit of Albert Clements.

Answer of Williams and Pounds.

Order making Edison Electric Illuminating Company and Amsterdam Electric Light, Heat and Power Company Parties Defendant.

Answer of Edison Electric Illuminating Company—in opposition to motion.

Exhibit "A"—annexed to answer of Edison Company (franchises of Municipal Electric Light Company and Citizens' Electric Illuminating Company of Brooklyn).

Exhibit "B"—(certificate of incorporation of Municipal Electric Light Company).

Exhibit "C"—(certificate of incorporation of Citizens' Electric Illuminating Company of Brooklyn).

Exhibit "D"—(certificate of incorporation of Edison Electric Illuminating Company of Brooklyn).

Exhibit "E"—(franchise of Edison Electric Illuminating Company of Brooklyn).

Exhibit "F"—(contract and specifications for furnishing electric lighting in the year 1895, the contracting parties being the city of Brooklyn and the Citizens Electric Illuminating Company).

Exhibit "G"—(contract and specifications for furnishing electric lighting in the year 1896, the contracting parties being the city of Brooklyn and the Citizens Electric Illuminating Company).

Exhibit "H"—(contract and specifications for furnishing electric lighting in the year 1897, the contracting parties being the city of Brooklyn and the Citizens Electric Illuminating Company).

Exhibit "I"—(Edison Company's certification to merger into itself of the Municipal Electric Light Company).

Exhibit "J"—(Edison Company's certification to merger into itself of the Citizens Electric Illuminating Company of Brooklyn).

Exhibit "K"—(certificate of incorporation of Kings County Electric Light and Power Company).

Exhibit "L"—(franchise of Kings County Electric Light and Power Company).

Exhibit "M"—(franchise of State Electric Light and Power Company and Amsterdam Electric Light, Heat and Power Company).

Exhibit "N"—(certificate of incorporation of Amsterdam Electric Light, Heat and Power Company).

Answer of Amsterdam Electric Light, Heat and Power Company.

Exhibit "A"—annexed to answer of Amsterdam Company (franchise of State Electric Light and Power Company and Amsterdam Electric Light, Heat and Power Company).

Exhibit "B"—(certificate of incorporation of Amsterdam Electric Light, Heat and Power Company).

Affidavit of William P. Burr, attorney for petitioner.

Affidavit of Samuel P. Moran, one of the attorneys for the Edison and Amsterdam companies.

Judgment—annexed to affidavit of Samuel P. Moran.

Affidavit of Vincent Victory, Deputy Assistant Corporation Counsel

Judgment, annexed to affidavit of Vincent Victory.

Opinion of Mr. Justice Benedict.

IV. Documents on Merger and Bond Issue

Petition of the Kings County Electric Light and Power Company for permission and approval of the Commission to merge the Edison Electric Illuminating Company of Brooklyn into and with itself and to execute a mortgage on its plant and property. (Case No. 2351).

Minutes of Hearing on Case No. 2351 (application for permission to merge and for approval of mortgage), December 16, 1918.

Minutes of Hearing on Case No. 2351, December 23, 1918.

Order authorizing merger and consenting to mortgage (in Case No. 2351), January 27, 1919.

Memorandum by Commissioner F. J. H. Kracke, February 3, 1919, upon granting application to merge and to execute mortgage.

Copy of mortgage of the Brooklyn Edison Company, Inc., to the Central Union Trust Company of New York, as trustee, dated January 1, 1919.

Petition of the Kings County Electric Light and Power Company, asking for authority to issue $6,000,000 worth of bonds.

Minutes of Hearing on Case No. 2352 (issuance of bonds), December 30, 1918.

Minutes of Hearing on Case No. 2352, January 9, 1919.

Minutes of Hearing on Case No. 2352, January 16, 1919.

Minutes of Hearing on Case No. 2352, January 23, 1919.

Minutes of Hearing on Case No. 2352, January 24, 1919.

Order authorizing issuance of $5,500,000 of bonds (in Case No. 2352), January 27, 1919.

Memorandum by Commissioner F. J. H. Kracke, February 3, 1919, upon authorizing the issuance of $5,500,000 of bonds.

Answer of the City of New York in the matter of the petition of the Kings County Electric Light and Power Company for the permission and approval of the Public Service Commission of the State of New York for the First District to merge the Edison Electric Illuminating Company of Brooklyn into and with itself and to execute a general mortgage to be designated as its "general mortgage" upon all its plan and property.

VITA

The writer was born on January 4, 1883, at Badger, Iowa. She completed two years of the college course at State Teachers College, Cedar Falls, Iowa, in 1911, receiving the diploma Bachelor of Didactics. She was graduated from Iowa State University, Iowa City, Iowa, in 1916 with the B. A. degree; and in 1917 with the M. A. degree. During the next two years she continued her work in the field of economics at Columbia University. Courses were attended at Columbia given by Professors R. E. Chaddock, F. H. Giddings, H. L. McBain, W. C. Mitchell, E. R. A. Seligman and V. G. Simkhovitch. She attended seminars conducted by Professors W. C. Mitchell, E. R. A. Seligman and V. G. Simkhovitch.

She has held the following positions: Head of the English department, Waldorf College, Forest City, Iowa, 1911-14; Assistant in the department of Economics, Iowa State University, 1916-1917; Supervisor of Normal Training summer sessions in Mount St. Joseph, Ottumwa, Iowa, summer of 1915, and in Mount St. Mary, Cherokee, Iowa, summer of 1916; Assistant Supervisor of Normal Training Session, Dubuque College, Dubuque, Iowa, summers of 1917, 1918 and 1919. She is a member of the Phi Beta Kappa fraternity.

www.ingramcontent.com/pod-product-compliance
Lightning Source LLC
LaVergne TN
LVHW011225110826
845150LV00006B/1546

9781425515621